Baby Care

MW00954178

Laura Rizer

ISBN-13:
978-1724676061

ISBN-10:
1724676067

"I don't know how you did it. I'm overwhelmed with just one!"

When my twins were babies, this is what I often heard when I met other new moms. And to be completely honest, looking back 4 years later, sometimes I am not sure myself. Being a first time mother to two babies at the same time is exhausting, draining, and frankly scary. But was also amazing, empowering, and I wouldn't trade it for any other experience in the world.

Now that I find myself in the role of "experienced mom" I'm so happy that I can take a few of the lessons that I learned with my twins to help keep my friends from becoming overwhelmed. I've shared my #1 secret with them, and now I'm sharing it with you too.

KEEPING A DAILY BABY LOG

When you become a mom, it's more important than ever to get organized. It's the way I keep from becoming overwhelmed and overstressed when it comes to life with kids.

When my twins were babies, keeping a daily baby log was an absolute necessity. Even if you have a singleton, a daily baby log will help you to keep a record of your baby's care and to help you keep things straight in the exhausting early days, weeks, and even months. The baby care log is perfect for moms, caregivers, and even makes a great gift.

This baby care journal will help you track baby's day and makes a great record for you to share with doctors or other caregivers. I remember when my boys were tiny and our doctor would ask how much they were eating, how many diapers they were going through, etc. My sleep deprived brain was so fogged (and I was keeping track of two) that it was so awesome to just hand her my log sheets and know I was giving her the right information. And it's a fun record to go back and look through (I just peeked through ours again).

The baby care journal includes spaces to record:

- Feeding Times & Amounts. There is space for both breast and bottle feeding (I did both).
- Diaper Changes. Simply check "wet" or "dirty" to keep a running count.
- Sleep & Nap Times. Track the start and end times of baby's naps and sleep.
- Tummy Time. Include the start and end time (I had one baby that hated tummy time and one that loved it).
- Medications. Keep a record of medication, dosage, and time given.
- Notes. A fun place to record any milestones or things you want to remember.

You'll find enough pages to record all of baby's first year (or 6 months for twins). If you're using it for multiples, simply use one page per baby and record his or her name on the top of each page.

And remember mama, you've got this.

Baby Care Journal
A Daily Record of Baby's Needs

BABY CARE JOURNAL

NAME: _____   DATE: _____

FEEDING

TIME	BREAST (TIME)	L / R	BOTTLE (OZ.)

DIAPERS

WET	DIRTY
☐	☐
☐	☐
☐	☐
☐	☐
☐	☐
☐	☐
☐	☐
☐	☐

TUMMY TIME

START TIME	END TIME

SLEEP/NAPS

START TIME	END TIME

MEDICATIONS

TIME	NAME & DOSAGE

NOTES

Baby Care Journal

NAME: _____ DATE: _____

Feeding

Time	Breast (Time)	L / R	Bottle (oz.)

Diapers

Wet	Dirty
☐	☐
☐	☐
☐	☐
☐	☐
☐	☐
☐	☐
☐	☐
☐	☐

Tummy Time

Start Time	End Time

Sleep/Naps

Start Time	End Time

Medications

Time	Name & Dosage

Notes

BABY CARE JOURNAL

NAME: _____   DATE: _____

FEEDING

Time	Breast (Time)	L / R	Bottle (oz.)

DIAPERS

Wet	Dirty
☐	☐
☐	☐
☐	☐
☐	☐
☐	☐
☐	☐
☐	☐
☐	☐

TUMMY TIME

Start Time	End Time

SLEEP/NAPS

Start Time	End Time

MEDICATIONS

Time	Name & Dosage

NOTES

BABY CARE JOURNAL

NAME: _____   DATE: _____

FEEDING

TIME	BREAST (TIME)	L / R	BOTTLE (OZ.)

DIAPERS

WET	DIRTY
☐	☐
☐	☐
☐	☐
☐	☐
☐	☐
☐	☐
☐	☐

TUMMY TIME

START TIME	END TIME

SLEEP/NAPS

START TIME	END TIME

MEDICATIONS

TIME	NAME & DOSAGE

NOTES

Baby Care Journal

Name: _____   Date: _____

Feeding

Time	Breast (Time)	L / R	Bottle (oz.)

Diapers

Wet	Dirty
☐	☐
☐	☐
☐	☐
☐	☐
☐	☐
☐	☐
☐	☐
☐	☐

Tummy Time

Start Time	End Time

Sleep/Naps

Start Time	End Time

Medications

Time	Name & Dosage

Notes

BABY CARE JOURNAL

NAME: _____   DATE: _____

FEEDING

TIME	BREAST (TIME)	L / R	BOTTLE (OZ.)

DIAPERS

WET	DIRTY
☐	☐
☐	☐
☐	☐
☐	☐
☐	☐
☐	☐
☐	☐
☐	☐

TUMMY TIME

START TIME	END TIME

SLEEP/NAPS

START TIME	END TIME

MEDICATIONS

TIME	NAME & DOSAGE

NOTES

BABY CARE JOURNAL

NAME: _____   DATE: _____

FEEDING

TIME	BREAST (TIME)	L / R	BOTTLE (OZ.)

DIAPERS

WET	DIRTY

TUMMY TIME

START TIME	END TIME

SLEEP/NAPS

START TIME	END TIME

MEDICATIONS

TIME	NAME & DOSAGE

NOTES

Baby Care Journal

Name: _____   Date: _____

Feeding

Time	Breast (Time)	L / R	Bottle (oz.)

Diapers

Wet	Dirty
☐	☐
☐	☐
☐	☐
☐	☐
☐	☐
☐	☐
☐	☐
☐	☐

Tummy Time

Start Time	End Time

Sleep/Naps

Start Time	End Time

Medications

Time	Name & Dosage

Notes

BABY CARE JOURNAL

NAME: _____   DATE: _____

FEEDING

Time	Breast (Time)	L / R	Bottle (Oz.)

DIAPERS

Wet	Dirty
☐	☐
☐	☐
☐	☐
☐	☐
☐	☐
☐	☐
☐	☐
☐	☐

TUMMY TIME

Start Time	End Time

SLEEP/NAPS

Start Time	End Time

MEDICATIONS

Time	Name & Dosage

NOTES

BABY CARE JOURNAL

NAME: _____   DATE: _____

FEEDING

Time	Breast (Time)	L / R	Bottle (oz.)

DIAPERS

Wet	Dirty
☐	☐
☐	☐
☐	☐
☐	☐
☐	☐
☐	☐
☐	☐
☐	☐

TUMMY TIME

Start Time	End Time

SLEEP/NAPS

Start Time	End Time

MEDICATIONS

Time	Name & Dosage

NOTES

Baby Care Journal

Name: _____ Date: _____

Feeding

Time	Breast (Time) L / R	Bottle (oz.)

Diapers

Wet	Dirty
☐	☐
☐	☐
☐	☐
☐	☐
☐	☐
☐	☐
☐	☐
☐	☐

Tummy Time

Start Time	End Time

Sleep/Naps

Start Time	End Time

Medications

Time	Name & Dosage

Notes

BABY CARE JOURNAL

NAME: _____   DATE: _____

FEEDING

TIME	BREAST (TIME)	L / R	BOTTLE (OZ.)

DIAPERS

WET	DIRTY

TUMMY TIME

START TIME	END TIME

SLEEP/NAPS

START TIME	END TIME

MEDICATIONS

TIME	NAME & DOSAGE

NOTES

BABY CARE JOURNAL

NAME: _____   DATE: _____

FEEDING

Time	Breast (Time)	L / R	Bottle (oz.)

DIAPERS

Wet	Dirty
☐	☐
☐	☐
☐	☐
☐	☐
☐	☐
☐	☐
☐	☐
☐	☐

TUMMY TIME

Start Time	End Time

SLEEP/NAPS

Start Time	End Time

MEDICATIONS

Time	Name & Dosage

NOTES

Baby Care Journal

Name: _____ Date: _____

Feeding

Time	Breast (Time)	L / R	Bottle (oz.)

Diapers

Wet	Dirty

Tummy Time

Start Time	End Time

Sleep/Naps

Start Time	End Time

Medications

Time	Name & Dosage

Notes

BABY CARE JOURNAL

NAME: _____   DATE: _____

FEEDING

TIME	BREAST (TIME)	L / R	BOTTLE (OZ.)

DIAPERS

WET	DIRTY
☐	☐
☐	☐
☐	☐
☐	☐
☐	☐
☐	☐
☐	☐

TUMMY TIME

START TIME	END TIME

SLEEP/NAPS

START TIME	END TIME

MEDICATIONS

TIME	NAME & DOSAGE

NOTES

BABY CARE JOURNAL

NAME: _____   DATE: _____

FEEDING

Time	Breast (Time)	L/R	Bottle (oz.)

DIAPERS

Wet	Dirty
☐	☐
☐	☐
☐	☐
☐	☐
☐	☐
☐	☐
☐	☐

TUMMY TIME

Start Time	End Time

SLEEP/NAPS

Start Time	End Time

MEDICATIONS

Time	Name & Dosage

NOTES

Baby Care Journal

NAME: _____   DATE: _____

Feeding

Time	Breast (Time)	L / R	Bottle (oz.)

Diapers

Wet	Dirty
☐	☐
☐	☐
☐	☐
☐	☐
☐	☐
☐	☐
☐	☐
☐	☐

Tummy Time

Start Time	End Time

Sleep/Naps

Start Time	End Time

Medications

Time	Name & Dosage

Notes

BABY CARE JOURNAL

NAME: _____   DATE: _____

FEEDING

TIME	BREAST (TIME)	L / R	BOTTLE (OZ.)

DIAPERS

WET	DIRTY

TUMMY TIME

START TIME	END TIME

SLEEP/NAPS

START TIME	END TIME

MEDICATIONS

TIME	NAME & DOSAGE

NOTES

BABY CARE JOURNAL

NAME: _____   DATE: _____

FEEDING

TIME	BREAST (TIME)	L / R	BOTTLE (OZ.)

DIAPERS

WET	DIRTY
☐	☐
☐	☐
☐	☐
☐	☐
☐	☐
☐	☐
☐	☐
☐	☐

TUMMY TIME

START TIME	END TIME

SLEEP/NAPS

START TIME	END TIME

MEDICATIONS

TIME	NAME & DOSAGE

NOTES

Baby Care Journal

NAME: _____   DATE: _____

FEEDING

Time	Breast (Time)	L / R	Bottle (oz.)

DIAPERS

Wet	Dirty
☐	☐
☐	☐
☐	☐
☐	☐
☐	☐
☐	☐
☐	☐
☐	☐

TUMMY TIME

Start Time	End Time

SLEEP/NAPS

Start Time	End Time

MEDICATIONS

Time	Name & Dosage

NOTES

Baby Care Journal

Name: _____   Date: _____

Feeding

Time	Breast (Time)	L / R	Bottle (Oz.)

Diapers

Wet	Dirty
☐	☐
☐	☐
☐	☐
☐	☐
☐	☐
☐	☐
☐	☐
☐	☐

Tummy Time

Start Time	End Time

Sleep/Naps

Start Time	End Time

Medications

Time	Name & Dosage

Notes

BABY CARE JOURNAL

NAME: _____ DATE: _____

FEEDING

TIME	BREAST (TIME)	L / R	BOTTLE (OZ.)

DIAPERS

WET	DIRTY
☐	☐
☐	☐
☐	☐
☐	☐
☐	☐
☐	☐
☐	☐
☐	☐

TUMMY TIME

START TIME	END TIME

SLEEP/NAPS

START TIME	END TIME

MEDICATIONS

TIME	NAME & DOSAGE

NOTES

BABY CARE JOURNAL

NAME: _____   DATE: _____

FEEDING

TIME	BREAST (TIME)	L / R	BOTTLE (OZ.)

DIAPERS

WET	DIRTY
☐	☐
☐	☐
☐	☐
☐	☐
☐	☐
☐	☐
☐	☐

TUMMY TIME

START TIME	END TIME

SLEEP/NAPS

START TIME	END TIME

MEDICATIONS

TIME	NAME & DOSAGE

NOTES

Baby Care Journal

Name: _____   Date: _____

Feeding

Time	Breast (Time)	L / R	Bottle (oz.)

Diapers

Wet	Dirty
☐	☐
☐	☐
☐	☐
☐	☐
☐	☐
☐	☐
☐	☐
☐	☐
☐	☐

Tummy Time

Start Time	End Time

Sleep/Naps

Start Time	End Time

Medications

Time	Name & Dosage

Notes

Baby Care Journal

NAME: _____ DATE: _____

Feeding

Time	Breast (Time)	L / R	Bottle (oz.)

Diapers

Wet	Dirty
☐	☐
☐	☐
☐	☐
☐	☐
☐	☐
☐	☐
☐	☐
☐	☐

Tummy Time

Start Time	End Time

Sleep/Naps

Start Time	End Time

Medications

Time	Name & Dosage

Notes

Baby Care Journal

Name: _____   Date: _____

Feeding

Time	Breast (Time)	L / R	Bottle (oz.)

Diapers

Wet	Dirty
☐	☐
☐	☐
☐	☐
☐	☐
☐	☐
☐	☐
☐	☐
☐	☐

Tummy Time

Start Time	End Time

Sleep/Naps

Start Time	End Time

Medications

Time	Name & Dosage

Notes

Baby Care Journal

Name: _____   Date: _____

Feeding

Time	Breast (Time)	L / R	Bottle (Oz.)

Diapers

Wet	Dirty
☐	☐
☐	☐
☐	☐
☐	☐
☐	☐
☐	☐
☐	☐
☐	☐

Tummy Time

Start Time	End Time

Sleep/Naps

Start Time	End Time

Medications

Time	Name & Dosage

Notes

BABY CARE JOURNAL

NAME: _____   DATE: _____

FEEDING

Time	Breast (Time)	L / R	Bottle (oz.)

DIAPERS

Wet	Dirty
☐	☐
☐	☐
☐	☐
☐	☐
☐	☐
☐	☐
☐	☐

TUMMY TIME

Start Time	End Time

SLEEP/NAPS

Start Time	End Time

MEDICATIONS

Time	Name & Dosage

NOTES

Baby Care Journal

NAME: _____   DATE: _____

Feeding

Time	Breast (Time)	L / R	Bottle (oz.)

Diapers

Wet	Dirty
☐	☐
☐	☐
☐	☐
☐	☐
☐	☐
☐	☐
☐	☐
☐	☐

Tummy Time

Start Time	End Time

Sleep/Naps

Start Time	End Time

Medications

Time	Name & Dosage

Notes

Baby Care Journal

Name: _____   Date: _____

Feeding

Time	Breast (Time)	L / R	Bottle (oz.)

Diapers

Wet	Dirty
☐	☐
☐	☐
☐	☐
☐	☐
☐	☐
☐	☐
☐	☐

Tummy Time

Start Time	End Time

Sleep/Naps

Start Time	End Time

Medications

Time	Name & Dosage

Notes

Baby Care Journal

NAME: _____   DATE: _____

Feeding

Time	Breast (Time)	L / R	Bottle (oz.)

Diapers

Wet	Dirty
☐	☐
☐	☐
☐	☐
☐	☐
☐	☐
☐	☐
☐	☐
☐	☐

Tummy Time

Start Time	End Time

Sleep/Naps

Start Time	End Time

Medications

Time	Name & Dosage

Notes

Baby Care Journal

Name: _____   Date: _____

Feeding

Time	Breast (Time)	L / R	Bottle (oz.)

Diapers

Wet	Dirty
☐	☐
☐	☐
☐	☐
☐	☐
☐	☐
☐	☐
☐	☐
☐	☐

Tummy Time

Start Time	End Time

Sleep/Naps

Start Time	End Time

Medications

Time	Name & Dosage

Notes

Baby Care Journal

NAME: _____   DATE: _____

Feeding

Time	Breast (Time)	L / R	Bottle (oz.)

Diapers

Wet	Dirty
☐	☐
☐	☐
☐	☐
☐	☐
☐	☐
☐	☐
☐	☐
☐	☐

Tummy Time

Start Time	End Time

Sleep/Naps

Start Time	End Time

Medications

Time	Name & Dosage

Notes

BABY CARE JOURNAL

NAME: _____ DATE: _____

FEEDING

TIME	BREAST (TIME)	L / R	BOTTLE (OZ.)

DIAPERS

WET	DIRTY
☐	☐
☐	☐
☐	☐
☐	☐
☐	☐
☐	☐
☐	☐
☐	☐

TUMMY TIME

START TIME	END TIME

SLEEP/NAPS

START TIME	END TIME

MEDICATIONS

TIME	NAME & DOSAGE

NOTES

Baby Care Journal

Name: _____   Date: _____

Feeding

Time	Breast (Time)	L / R	Bottle (oz.)

Diapers

Wet	Dirty

Tummy Time

Start Time	End Time

Sleep/Naps

Start Time	End Time

Medications

Time	Name & Dosage

Notes

Baby Care Journal

Name: _____   Date: _____

Feeding

Time	Breast (Time)	L / R	Bottle (oz.)

Diapers

Wet	Dirty
☐	☐
☐	☐
☐	☐
☐	☐
☐	☐
☐	☐
☐	☐
☐	☐

Tummy Time

Start Time	End Time

Sleep/Naps

Start Time	End Time

Medications

Time	Name & Dosage

Notes

BABY CARE JOURNAL

NAME: _____ DATE: _____

FEEDING

Time	Breast (Time)	L / R	Bottle (oz.)

DIAPERS

Wet	Dirty
☐	☐
☐	☐
☐	☐
☐	☐
☐	☐
☐	☐
☐	☐

TUMMY TIME

Start Time	End Time

SLEEP/NAPS

Start Time	End Time

MEDICATIONS

Time	Name & Dosage

NOTES

BABY CARE JOURNAL

NAME: _____   DATE: _____

FEEDING

Time	Breast (Time)	L / R	Bottle (oz.)

DIAPERS

Wet	Dirty
☐	☐
☐	☐
☐	☐
☐	☐
☐	☐
☐	☐
☐	☐
☐	☐

TUMMY TIME

Start Time	End Time

SLEEP/NAPS

Start Time	End Time

MEDICATIONS

Time	Name & Dosage

NOTES

Baby Care Journal

NAME: _____ DATE: _____

FEEDING

Time	Breast (Time)	L / R	Bottle (Oz.)

DIAPERS

Wet	Dirty
☐	☐
☐	☐
☐	☐
☐	☐
☐	☐
☐	☐
☐	☐
☐	☐

TUMMY TIME

Start Time	End Time

SLEEP/NAPS

Start Time	End Time

MEDICATIONS

Time	Name & Dosage

NOTES

BABY CARE JOURNAL

NAME: _____   DATE: _____

FEEDING

Time	Breast (Time)	L / R	Bottle (oz.)

DIAPERS

Wet	Dirty
☐	☐
☐	☐
☐	☐
☐	☐
☐	☐
☐	☐
☐	☐
☐	☐

TUMMY TIME

Start Time	End Time

SLEEP/NAPS

Start Time	End Time

MEDICATIONS

Time	Name & Dosage

NOTES

BABY CARE JOURNAL

NAME: _____   DATE: _____

FEEDING

Time	Breast (Time)	L / R	Bottle (oz.)

DIAPERS

Wet	Dirty
☐	☐
☐	☐
☐	☐
☐	☐
☐	☐
☐	☐
☐	☐
☐	☐

TUMMY TIME

Start Time	End Time

SLEEP/NAPS

Start Time	End Time

MEDICATIONS

Time	Name & Dosage

NOTES

BABY CARE JOURNAL

NAME: _____   DATE: _____

FEEDING

TIME	BREAST (TIME)	L / R	BOTTLE (OZ.)

DIAPERS

WET	DIRTY

TUMMY TIME

START TIME	END TIME

SLEEP/NAPS

START TIME	END TIME

MEDICATIONS

TIME	NAME & DOSAGE

NOTES

Baby Care Journal

NAME: _____   DATE: _____

FEEDING

Time	Breast (Time)	L / R	Bottle (oz.)

DIAPERS

Wet	Dirty
☐	☐
☐	☐
☐	☐
☐	☐
☐	☐
☐	☐
☐	☐
☐	☐

TUMMY TIME

Start Time	End Time

SLEEP/NAPS

Start Time	End Time

MEDICATIONS

Time	Name & Dosage

NOTES

Baby Care Journal

NAME: _____   DATE: _____

FEEDING

Time	Breast (Time)	L / R	Bottle (oz.)

DIAPERS

Wet	Dirty
☐	☐
☐	☐
☐	☐
☐	☐
☐	☐
☐	☐
☐	☐
☐	☐

TUMMY TIME

Start Time	End Time

SLEEP/NAPS

Start Time	End Time

MEDICATIONS

Time	Name & Dosage

NOTES

Baby Care Journal

Name: _____ Date: _____

Feeding

Time	Breast (Time)	L / R	Bottle (Oz.)

Diapers

Wet	Dirty

Tummy Time

Start Time	End Time

Sleep/Naps

Start Time	End Time

Medications

Time	Name & Dosage

Notes

BABY CARE JOURNAL

NAME: _____   DATE: _____

FEEDING

Time	BREAST (Time)	L / R	BOTTLE (OZ.)

DIAPERS

Wet	Dirty
☐	☐
☐	☐
☐	☐
☐	☐
☐	☐
☐	☐
☐	☐
☐	☐

TUMMY TIME

START TIME	END TIME

SLEEP/NAPS

START TIME	END TIME

MEDICATIONS

TIME	NAME & DOSAGE

NOTES

BABY CARE JOURNAL

NAME: _____   DATE: _____

FEEDING

Time	Breast (Time)	L / R	Bottle (Oz.)

DIAPERS

Wet	Dirty
☐	☐
☐	☐
☐	☐
☐	☐
☐	☐
☐	☐
☐	☐
☐	☐

TUMMY TIME

Start Time	End Time

SLEEP/NAPS

Start Time	End Time

MEDICATIONS

Time	Name & Dosage

NOTES

BABY CARE JOURNAL

NAME: _____   DATE: _____

FEEDING

TIME	BREAST (TIME)	L / R	BOTTLE (OZ.)

DIAPERS

WET	DIRTY
☐	☐
☐	☐
☐	☐
☐	☐
☐	☐
☐	☐
☐	☐
☐	☐

TUMMY TIME

START TIME	END TIME

SLEEP/NAPS

START TIME	END TIME

MEDICATIONS

TIME	NAME & DOSAGE

NOTES

Baby Care Journal

Name: _____   Date: _____

Feeding

Time	Breast (Time)	L / R	Bottle (oz.)

Diapers

Wet	Dirty

Tummy Time

Start Time	End Time

Sleep/Naps

Start Time	End Time

Medications

Time	Name & Dosage

Notes

BABY CARE JOURNAL

NAME: _____ DATE: _____

FEEDING

TIME	BREAST (TIME)	L / R	BOTTLE (OZ.)

DIAPERS

WET	DIRTY
☐	☐
☐	☐
☐	☐
☐	☐
☐	☐
☐	☐
☐	☐
☐	☐

TUMMY TIME

START TIME	END TIME

SLEEP/NAPS

START TIME	END TIME

MEDICATIONS

TIME	NAME & DOSAGE

NOTES

BABY CARE JOURNAL

NAME: _____   DATE: _____

FEEDING

Time	Breast (Time)	L / R	Bottle (oz.)

DIAPERS

Wet	Dirty
☐	☐
☐	☐
☐	☐
☐	☐
☐	☐
☐	☐
☐	☐
☐	☐

TUMMY TIME

Start Time	End Time

SLEEP/NAPS

Start Time	End Time

MEDICATIONS

Time	Name & Dosage

NOTES

BABY CARE JOURNAL

NAME: _____   DATE: _____

FEEDING

TIME	BREAST (TIME)	L / R	BOTTLE (OZ.)

DIAPERS

WET	DIRTY

TUMMY TIME

START TIME	END TIME

SLEEP/NAPS

START TIME	END TIME

MEDICATIONS

TIME	NAME & DOSAGE

NOTES

BABY CARE JOURNAL

NAME: _____ DATE: _____

FEEDING

TIME	BREAST (TIME)	L / R	BOTTLE (OZ.)

DIAPERS

WET	DIRTY
☐	☐
☐	☐
☐	☐
☐	☐
☐	☐
☐	☐
☐	☐
☐	☐

TUMMY TIME

START TIME	END TIME

SLEEP/NAPS

START TIME	END TIME

MEDICATIONS

TIME	NAME & DOSAGE

NOTES

BABY CARE JOURNAL

NAME: _____   DATE: _____

FEEDING

TIME	BREAST (TIME)	L / R	BOTTLE (OZ.)

DIAPERS

WET	DIRTY
☐	☐
☐	☐
☐	☐
☐	☐
☐	☐
☐	☐
☐	☐
☐	☐

TUMMY TIME

START TIME	END TIME

SLEEP/NAPS

START TIME	END TIME

MEDICATIONS

TIME	NAME & DOSAGE

NOTES

Baby Care Journal

NAME: _____ DATE: _____

FEEDING

Time	Breast (Time)	L / R	Bottle (oz.)

DIAPERS

Wet	Dirty
☐	☐
☐	☐
☐	☐
☐	☐
☐	☐
☐	☐
☐	☐
☐	☐

TUMMY TIME

Start Time	End Time

SLEEP/NAPS

Start Time	End Time

MEDICATIONS

Time	Name & Dosage

NOTES

Baby Care Journal

Name: _____ Date: _____

Feeding

Time	Breast (Time)	L / R	Bottle (oz.)

Diapers

Wet	Dirty
☐	☐
☐	☐
☐	☐
☐	☐
☐	☐
☐	☐
☐	☐
☐	☐

Tummy Time

Start Time	End Time

Sleep/Naps

Start Time	End Time

Medications

Time	Name & Dosage

Notes

BABY CARE JOURNAL

NAME: _____   DATE: _____

FEEDING

TIME	BREAST (TIME)	L / R	BOTTLE (OZ.)

DIAPERS

WET	DIRTY

TUMMY TIME

START TIME	END TIME

SLEEP/NAPS

START TIME	END TIME

MEDICATIONS

TIME	NAME & DOSAGE

NOTES

Baby Care Journal

Name: _____   Date: _____

Feeding

Time	Breast (Time)	L / R	Bottle (oz.)

Diapers

Wet	Dirty

Tummy Time

Start Time	End Time

Sleep/Naps

Start Time	End Time

Medications

Time	Name & Dosage

Notes

Baby Care Journal

Name: _____   Date: _____

Feeding

Time	Breast (Time) L / R	Bottle (oz.)

Diapers

Wet	Dirty
☐	☐
☐	☐
☐	☐
☐	☐
☐	☐
☐	☐
☐	☐
☐	☐

Tummy Time

Start Time	End Time

Sleep/Naps

Start Time	End Time

Medications

Time	Name & Dosage

Notes

BABY CARE JOURNAL

NAME: _____   DATE: _____

FEEDING

TIME	BREAST (TIME)	L / R	BOTTLE (OZ.)

DIAPERS

WET	DIRTY
☐	☐
☐	☐
☐	☐
☐	☐
☐	☐
☐	☐
☐	☐
☐	☐

TUMMY TIME

START TIME	END TIME

SLEEP/NAPS

START TIME	END TIME

MEDICATIONS

TIME	NAME & DOSAGE

NOTES

Baby Care Journal

Name: _____ Date: _____

Feeding

Time	Breast (Time)	L / R	Bottle (oz.)

Diapers

Wet	Dirty
☐	☐
☐	☐
☐	☐
☐	☐
☐	☐
☐	☐
☐	☐
☐	☐

Tummy Time

Start Time	End Time

Sleep/Naps

Start Time	End Time

Medications

Time	Name & Dosage

Notes

BABY CARE JOURNAL

NAME: _____   DATE: _____

FEEDING

TIME	BREAST (TIME)	L / R	BOTTLE (OZ.)

DIAPERS

WET	DIRTY

TUMMY TIME

START TIME	END TIME

SLEEP/NAPS

START TIME	END TIME

MEDICATIONS

TIME	NAME & DOSAGE

NOTES

BABY CARE JOURNAL

NAME: _____   DATE: _____

FEEDING

Time	Breast (Time)	L / R	Bottle (oz.)

DIAPERS

Wet	Dirty

TUMMY TIME

Start Time	End Time

SLEEP/NAPS

Start Time	End Time

MEDICATIONS

Time	Name & Dosage

NOTES

Baby Care Journal

Name: _____   Date: _____

Feeding

Time	Breast (Time)	L / R	Bottle (Oz.)

Diapers

Wet	Dirty
☐	☐
☐	☐
☐	☐
☐	☐
☐	☐
☐	☐
☐	☐
☐	☐

Tummy Time

Start Time	End Time

Sleep/Naps

Start Time	End Time

Medications

Time	Name & Dosage

Notes

Baby Care Journal

Name: _____   Date: _____

Feeding

Time	Breast (Time)	L / R	Bottle (oz.)

Diapers

Wet	Dirty
☐	☐
☐	☐
☐	☐
☐	☐
☐	☐
☐	☐
☐	☐
☐	☐

Tummy Time

Start Time	End Time

Sleep/Naps

Start Time	End Time

Medications

Time	Name & Dosage

Notes

BABY CARE JOURNAL

NAME: _____   DATE: _____

FEEDING

TIME	BREAST (TIME)	L / R	BOTTLE (OZ.)

DIAPERS

WET	DIRTY
☐	☐
☐	☐
☐	☐
☐	☐
☐	☐
☐	☐
☐	☐
☐	☐

TUMMY TIME

START TIME	END TIME

SLEEP/NAPS

START TIME	END TIME

MEDICATIONS

TIME	NAME & DOSAGE

NOTES

Baby Care Journal

Name: _____ Date: _____

Feeding

Time	Breast (Time)	L / R	Bottle (oz.)

Diapers

Wet	Dirty
☐	☐
☐	☐
☐	☐
☐	☐
☐	☐
☐	☐
☐	☐
☐	☐

Tummy Time

Start Time	End Time

Sleep/Naps

Start Time	End Time

Medications

Time	Name & Dosage

Notes

BABY CARE JOURNAL

NAME: _____   DATE: _____

FEEDING

Time	Breast (Time)	L / R	Bottle (oz.)

DIAPERS

Wet	Dirty
☐	☐
☐	☐
☐	☐
☐	☐
☐	☐
☐	☐
☐	☐
☐	☐

TUMMY TIME

Start Time	End Time

SLEEP/NAPS

Start Time	End Time

MEDICATIONS

Time	Name & Dosage

NOTES

Baby Care Journal

Name: _____ Date: _____

Feeding

Time	Breast (Time)	L / R	Bottle (oz.)

Diapers

Wet	Dirty

Tummy Time

Start Time	End Time

Sleep/Naps

Start Time	End Time

Medications

Time	Name & Dosage

Notes

Baby Care Journal

Name: _____ Date: _____

Feeding

Time	Breast (Time)	L / R	Bottle (oz.)

Diapers

Wet	Dirty
☐	☐
☐	☐
☐	☐
☐	☐
☐	☐
☐	☐
☐	☐

Tummy Time

Start Time	End Time

Sleep/Naps

Start Time	End Time

Medications

Time	Name & Dosage

Notes

Baby Care Journal

Name: _____   Date: _____

Feeding

Time	Breast (Time) L / R	Bottle (oz.)

Diapers

Wet	Dirty

Tummy Time

Start Time	End Time

Sleep/Naps

Start Time	End Time

Medications

Time	Name & Dosage

Notes

BABY CARE JOURNAL

NAME: _____ DATE: _____

FEEDING

Time	Breast (Time)	L / R	Bottle (oz.)

DIAPERS

Wet	Dirty
☐	☐
☐	☐
☐	☐
☐	☐
☐	☐
☐	☐
☐	☐

TUMMY TIME

Start Time	End Time

SLEEP/NAPS

Start Time	End Time

MEDICATIONS

Time	Name & Dosage

NOTES

Baby Care Journal

NAME: _____ DATE: _____

Feeding

Time	Breast (Time)	L / R	Bottle (oz.)

Diapers

Wet	Dirty
☐	☐
☐	☐
☐	☐
☐	☐
☐	☐
☐	☐
☐	☐
☐	☐

Tummy Time

Start Time	End Time

Sleep/Naps

Start Time	End Time

Medications

Time	Name & Dosage

Notes

Baby Care Journal

Name: _____   Date: _____

Feeding

Time	Breast (Time)	L / R	Bottle (oz.)

Diapers

Wet	Dirty
☐	☐
☐	☐
☐	☐
☐	☐
☐	☐
☐	☐
☐	☐

Tummy Time

Start Time	End Time

Sleep/Naps

Start Time	End Time

Medications

Time	Name & Dosage

Notes

BABY CARE JOURNAL

NAME: _____ DATE: _____

FEEDING

Time	Breast (Time)	L / R	Bottle (Oz.)

DIAPERS

Wet	Dirty

TUMMY TIME

Start Time	End Time

SLEEP/NAPS

Start Time	End Time

MEDICATIONS

Time	Name & Dosage

NOTES

Baby Care Journal

NAME: _____   DATE: _____

FEEDING

Time	Breast (Time)	L / R	Bottle (oz.)

DIAPERS

Wet	Dirty
☐	☐
☐	☐
☐	☐
☐	☐
☐	☐
☐	☐
☐	☐
☐	☐

TUMMY TIME

Start Time	End Time

SLEEP/NAPS

Start Time	End Time

MEDICATIONS

Time	Name & Dosage

NOTES

Baby Care Journal

Name: _____ Date: _____

Feeding

Time	Breast (Time)	L / R	Bottle (oz.)

Diapers

Wet	Dirty

Tummy Time

Start Time	End Time

Sleep/Naps

Start Time	End Time

Medications

Time	Name & Dosage

Notes

Baby Care Journal

Name: _____   Date: _____

Feeding

Time	Breast (Time)	L / R	Bottle (oz.)

Diapers

Wet	Dirty
☐	☐
☐	☐
☐	☐
☐	☐
☐	☐
☐	☐
☐	☐
☐	☐

Tummy Time

Start Time	End Time

Sleep/Naps

Start Time	End Time

Medications

Time	Name & Dosage

Notes

Baby Care Journal

Name: _____   Date: _____

Feeding

Time	Breast (Time)	L / R	Bottle (oz.)

Diapers

Wet	Dirty
☐	☐
☐	☐
☐	☐
☐	☐
☐	☐
☐	☐
☐	☐

Tummy Time

Start Time	End Time

Sleep/Naps

Start Time	End Time

Medications

Time	Name & Dosage

Notes

Baby Care Journal

Name: _____   Date: _____

Feeding

Time	Breast (Time)	L / R	Bottle (oz.)

Diapers

Wet	Dirty
☐	☐
☐	☐
☐	☐
☐	☐
☐	☐
☐	☐
☐	☐
☐	☐

Tummy Time

Start Time	End Time

Sleep/Naps

Start Time	End Time

Medications

Time	Name & Dosage

Notes

Baby Care Journal

Name: _____   Date: _____

Feeding

Time	Breast (Time)	L / R	Bottle (oz.)

Diapers

Wet	Dirty
☐	☐
☐	☐
☐	☐
☐	☐
☐	☐
☐	☐
☐	☐
☐	☐

Tummy Time

Start Time	End Time

Sleep/Naps

Start Time	End Time

Medications

Time	Name & Dosage

Notes

Baby Care Journal

Name: _____ Date: _____

Feeding

Time	Breast (Time)	L / R	Bottle (oz.)

Diapers

Wet	Dirty
☐	☐
☐	☐
☐	☐
☐	☐
☐	☐
☐	☐
☐	☐

Tummy Time

Start Time	End Time

Sleep/Naps

Start Time	End Time

Medications

Time	Name & Dosage

Notes

Baby Care Journal

NAME: _____   DATE: _____

FEEDING

Time	Breast (Time)	L / R	Bottle (Oz.)

DIAPERS

Wet	Dirty

TUMMY TIME

Start Time	End Time

SLEEP/NAPS

Start Time	End Time

MEDICATIONS

Time	Name & Dosage

NOTES

BABY CARE JOURNAL

NAME: _____   DATE: _____

FEEDING

TIME	BREAST (TIME)	L / R	BOTTLE (OZ.)

DIAPERS

WET	DIRTY
☐	☐
☐	☐
☐	☐
☐	☐
☐	☐
☐	☐
☐	☐
☐	☐

TUMMY TIME

START TIME	END TIME

SLEEP/NAPS

START TIME	END TIME

MEDICATIONS

TIME	NAME & DOSAGE

NOTES

Baby Care Journal

Name: _____   Date: _____

Feeding

Time	Breast (Time)	L / R	Bottle (oz.)

Diapers

Wet	Dirty
☐	☐
☐	☐
☐	☐
☐	☐
☐	☐
☐	☐
☐	☐
☐	☐

Tummy Time

Start Time	End Time

Sleep/Naps

Start Time	End Time

Medications

Time	Name & Dosage

Notes

Baby Care Journal

Name: _____ Date: _____

Feeding

Time	Breast (Time)	L / R	Bottle (oz.)

Diapers

Wet	Dirty
☐	☐
☐	☐
☐	☐
☐	☐
☐	☐
☐	☐
☐	☐
☐	☐

Tummy Time

Start Time	End Time

Sleep/Naps

Start Time	End Time

Medications

Time	Name & Dosage

Notes

Baby Care Journal

NAME: _____   DATE: _____

Feeding

Time	Breast (Time)	L / R	Bottle (oz.)

Diapers

Wet	Dirty
☐	☐
☐	☐
☐	☐
☐	☐
☐	☐
☐	☐
☐	☐
☐	☐

Tummy Time

Start Time	End Time

Sleep/Naps

Start Time	End Time

Medications

Time	Name & Dosage

Notes

BABY CARE JOURNAL

NAME: _____   DATE: _____

FEEDING

TIME	BREAST (TIME)	L / R	BOTTLE (OZ.)

DIAPERS

WET	DIRTY

TUMMY TIME

START TIME	END TIME

SLEEP/NAPS

START TIME	END TIME

MEDICATIONS

TIME	NAME & DOSAGE

NOTES

Baby Care Journal

Name: _____   Date: _____

Feeding

Time	Breast (Time)	L / R	Bottle (oz.)

Diapers

Wet	Dirty
☐	☐
☐	☐
☐	☐
☐	☐
☐	☐
☐	☐
☐	☐
☐	☐

Tummy Time

Start Time	End Time

Sleep/Naps

Start Time	End Time

Medications

Time	Name & Dosage

Notes

Baby Care Journal

Name: _____   Date: _____

Feeding

Time	Breast (Time)	L / R	Bottle (oz.)

Diapers

Wet	Dirty
☐	☐
☐	☐
☐	☐
☐	☐
☐	☐
☐	☐
☐	☐
☐	☐

Tummy Time

Start Time	End Time

Sleep/Naps

Start Time	End Time

Medications

Time	Name & Dosage

Notes

BABY CARE JOURNAL

NAME: _____   DATE: _____

FEEDING

Time	Breast (Time)	L / R	Bottle (oz.)

DIAPERS

Wet	Dirty
☐	☐
☐	☐
☐	☐
☐	☐
☐	☐
☐	☐
☐	☐
☐	☐

TUMMY TIME

Start Time	End Time

SLEEP/NAPS

Start Time	End Time

MEDICATIONS

Time	Name & Dosage

NOTES

Baby Care Journal

NAME: _____ DATE: _____

FEEDING

Time	Breast (Time)	L / R	Bottle (oz.)

DIAPERS

Wet	Dirty
☐	☐
☐	☐
☐	☐
☐	☐
☐	☐
☐	☐
☐	☐
☐	☐

TUMMY TIME

Start Time	End Time

SLEEP/NAPS

Start Time	End Time

MEDICATIONS

Time	Name & Dosage

NOTES

Baby Care Journal

Name: _____   Date: _____

Feeding

Time	Breast (Time)	L / R	Bottle (Oz.)

Diapers

Wet	Dirty

Tummy Time

Start Time	End Time

Sleep/Naps

Start Time	End Time

Medications

Time	Name & Dosage

Notes

BABY CARE JOURNAL

NAME: _____   DATE: _____

FEEDING

TIME	BREAST (TIME)	L / R	BOTTLE (OZ.)

DIAPERS

WET	DIRTY

TUMMY TIME

START TIME	END TIME

SLEEP/NAPS

START TIME	END TIME

MEDICATIONS

TIME	NAME & DOSAGE

NOTES

Baby Care Journal

Name: _____   Date: _____

Feeding

Time	Breast (Time)	L / R	Bottle (oz.)

Diapers

Wet	Dirty
☐	☐
☐	☐
☐	☐
☐	☐
☐	☐
☐	☐
☐	☐
☐	☐

Tummy Time

Start Time	End Time

Sleep/Naps

Start Time	End Time

Medications

Time	Name & Dosage

Notes

BABY CARE JOURNAL

NAME: _____   DATE: _____

FEEDING

Time	Breast (Time)	L / R	Bottle (oz.)

DIAPERS

Wet	Dirty
☐	☐
☐	☐
☐	☐
☐	☐
☐	☐
☐	☐
☐	☐
☐	☐

TUMMY TIME

Start Time	End Time

SLEEP/NAPS

Start Time	End Time

MEDICATIONS

Time	Name & Dosage

NOTES

Baby Care Journal

Name: _____ Date: _____

Feeding

Time	Breast (Time)	L / R	Bottle (oz.)

Diapers

Wet	Dirty

Tummy Time

Start Time	End Time

Sleep/Naps

Start Time	End Time

Medications

Time	Name & Dosage

Notes

BABY CARE JOURNAL

NAME: _____   DATE: _____

FEEDING

TIME	BREAST (TIME)	L / R	BOTTLE (OZ.)

DIAPERS

WET	DIRTY
☐	☐
☐	☐
☐	☐
☐	☐
☐	☐
☐	☐
☐	☐
☐	☐

TUMMY TIME

START TIME	END TIME

SLEEP/NAPS

START TIME	END TIME

MEDICATIONS

TIME	NAME & DOSAGE

NOTES

BABY CARE JOURNAL

NAME: _____ DATE: _____

FEEDING

Time	Breast (Time)	L / R	Bottle (oz.)

DIAPERS

Wet	Dirty
☐	☐
☐	☐
☐	☐
☐	☐
☐	☐
☐	☐
☐	☐
☐	☐

TUMMY TIME

Start Time	End Time

SLEEP/NAPS

Start Time	End Time

MEDICATIONS

Time	Name & Dosage

NOTES

Baby Care Journal

Name: _____   Date: _____

Feeding

Time	Breast (Time)	L / R	Bottle (oz.)

Diapers

Wet	Dirty
☐	☐
☐	☐
☐	☐
☐	☐
☐	☐
☐	☐
☐	☐
☐	☐

Tummy Time

Start Time	End Time

Sleep/Naps

Start Time	End Time

Medications

Time	Name & Dosage

Notes

Baby Care Journal

Name: _____   Date: _____

Feeding

Time	Breast (Time)	L / R	Bottle (oz.)

Diapers

Wet	Dirty

Tummy Time

Start Time	End Time

Sleep/Naps

Start Time	End Time

Medications

Time	Name & Dosage

Notes

BABY CARE JOURNAL

NAME: _____   DATE: _____

FEEDING

TIME	BREAST (TIME)	L / R	BOTTLE (OZ.)

DIAPERS

WET	DIRTY
☐	☐
☐	☐
☐	☐
☐	☐
☐	☐
☐	☐
☐	☐

TUMMY TIME

START TIME	END TIME

SLEEP/NAPS

START TIME	END TIME

MEDICATIONS

TIME	NAME & DOSAGE

NOTES

Baby Care Journal

NAME: _____   DATE: _____

FEEDING

Time	Breast (Time)	L / R	Bottle (oz.)

DIAPERS

Wet	Dirty
☐	☐
☐	☐
☐	☐
☐	☐
☐	☐
☐	☐
☐	☐
☐	☐

TUMMY TIME

Start Time	End Time

SLEEP/NAPS

Start Time	End Time

MEDICATIONS

Time	Name & Dosage

NOTES

Baby Care Journal

Name: _____   Date: _____

Feeding

Time	Breast (Time)	L / R	Bottle (Oz.)

Diapers

Wet	Dirty
☐	☐
☐	☐
☐	☐
☐	☐
☐	☐
☐	☐
☐	☐

Tummy Time

Start Time	End Time

Sleep/Naps

Start Time	End Time

Medications

Time	Name & Dosage

Notes

Baby Care Journal

Name: _____ Date: _____

Feeding

Time	Breast (Time)	L / R	Bottle (oz.)

Diapers

Wet	Dirty
☐	☐
☐	☐
☐	☐
☐	☐
☐	☐
☐	☐
☐	☐

Tummy Time

Start Time	End Time

Sleep/Naps

Start Time	End Time

Medications

Time	Name & Dosage

Notes

Baby Care Journal

Name: _____   Date: _____

Feeding

Time	Breast (Time)	L / R	Bottle (oz.)

Diapers

Wet	Dirty
☐	☐
☐	☐
☐	☐
☐	☐
☐	☐
☐	☐
☐	☐
☐	☐

Tummy Time

Start Time	End Time

Sleep/Naps

Start Time	End Time

Medications

Time	Name & Dosage

Notes

BABY CARE JOURNAL

NAME: _____   DATE: _____

FEEDING

Time	Breast (Time)	L / R	Bottle (oz.)

DIAPERS

Wet	Dirty
☐	☐
☐	☐
☐	☐
☐	☐
☐	☐
☐	☐
☐	☐
☐	☐

TUMMY TIME

Start Time	End Time

SLEEP/NAPS

Start Time	End Time

MEDICATIONS

Time	Name & Dosage

NOTES

Baby Care Journal

NAME: _____   DATE: _____

FEEDING

Time	Breast (Time)	L / R	Bottle (oz.)

DIAPERS

Wet	Dirty
☐	☐
☐	☐
☐	☐
☐	☐
☐	☐
☐	☐
☐	☐
☐	☐

TUMMY TIME

Start Time	End Time

SLEEP/NAPS

Start Time	End Time

MEDICATIONS

Time	Name & Dosage

NOTES

BABY CARE JOURNAL

NAME: _____   DATE: _____

FEEDING

TIME	BREAST (TIME)	L / R	BOTTLE (OZ.)

DIAPERS

WET	DIRTY

TUMMY TIME

START TIME	END TIME

SLEEP/NAPS

START TIME	END TIME

MEDICATIONS

TIME	NAME & DOSAGE

NOTES

Baby Care Journal

Name: _____   Date: _____

Feeding

Time	Breast (Time)	L / R	Bottle (Oz.)

Diapers

Wet	Dirty

Tummy Time

Start Time	End Time

Sleep/Naps

Start Time	End Time

Medications

Time	Name & Dosage

Notes

Baby Care Journal

NAME: _____ DATE: _____

Feeding

Time	Breast (Time)	L / R	Bottle (oz.)

Diapers

Wet	Dirty
☐	☐
☐	☐
☐	☐
☐	☐
☐	☐
☐	☐
☐	☐
☐	☐

Tummy Time

Start Time	End Time

Sleep/Naps

Start Time	End Time

Medications

Time	Name & Dosage

Notes

Baby Care Journal

Name: _____ Date: _____

Feeding

Time	Breast (Time)	L / R	Bottle (oz.)

Diapers

Wet	Dirty
☐	☐
☐	☐
☐	☐
☐	☐
☐	☐
☐	☐
☐	☐

Tummy Time

Start Time	End Time

Sleep/Naps

Start Time	End Time

Medications

Time	Name & Dosage

Notes

BABY CARE JOURNAL

NAME: _____ DATE: _____

FEEDING

TIME	BREAST (TIME)	L / R	BOTTLE (OZ.)

DIAPERS

WET	DIRTY

TUMMY TIME

START TIME	END TIME

SLEEP/NAPS

START TIME	END TIME

MEDICATIONS

TIME	NAME & DOSAGE

NOTES

BABY CARE JOURNAL

NAME: _____   DATE: _____

FEEDING

TIME	BREAST (TIME)	L / R	BOTTLE (OZ.)

DIAPERS

WET	DIRTY
☐	☐
☐	☐
☐	☐
☐	☐
☐	☐
☐	☐
☐	☐
☐	☐

TUMMY TIME

START TIME	END TIME

SLEEP/NAPS

START TIME	END TIME

MEDICATIONS

TIME	NAME & DOSAGE

NOTES

BABY CARE JOURNAL

NAME: _____   DATE: _____

FEEDING

Time	Breast (Time)	L / R	Bottle (oz.)

DIAPERS

Wet	Dirty
☐	☐
☐	☐
☐	☐
☐	☐
☐	☐
☐	☐
☐	☐
☐	

TUMMY TIME

Start Time	End Time

SLEEP/NAPS

Start Time	End Time

MEDICATIONS

Time	Name & Dosage

NOTES

Baby Care Journal

Name: _____ Date: _____

Feeding

Time	Breast (Time)	L / R	Bottle (oz.)

Diapers

Wet	Dirty
☐	☐
☐	☐
☐	☐
☐	☐
☐	☐
☐	☐
☐	☐
☐	☐

Tummy Time

Start Time	End Time

Sleep/Naps

Start Time	End Time

Medications

Time	Name & Dosage

Notes

Baby Care Journal

Name: _____ Date: _____

Feeding

Time	Breast (Time)	L / R	Bottle (oz.)

Diapers

Wet	Dirty

Tummy Time

Start Time	End Time

Sleep/Naps

Start Time	End Time

Medications

Time	Name & Dosage

Notes

Baby Care Journal

Name: _____   Date: _____

Feeding

Time	Breast (Time)	L / R	Bottle (oz.)

Diapers

Wet	Dirty
☐	☐
☐	☐
☐	☐
☐	☐
☐	☐
☐	☐
☐	☐
☐	☐

Tummy Time

Start Time	End Time

Sleep/Naps

Start Time	End Time

Medications

Time	Name & Dosage

Notes

BABY CARE JOURNAL

NAME: _____   DATE: _____

FEEDING

Time	Breast (Time)	L / R	Bottle (oz.)

DIAPERS

Wet	Dirty

TUMMY TIME

Start Time	End Time

SLEEP/NAPS

Start Time	End Time

MEDICATIONS

Time	Name & Dosage

NOTES

Baby Care Journal

Name: _____   Date: _____

Feeding

Time	Breast (Time)	L / R	Bottle (oz.)

Diapers

Wet	Dirty
☐	☐
☐	☐
☐	☐
☐	☐
☐	☐
☐	☐
☐	☐
☐	☐

Tummy Time

Start Time	End Time

Sleep/Naps

Start Time	End Time

Medications

Time	Name & Dosage

Notes

Baby Care Journal

Name: _____   Date: _____

Feeding

Time	Breast (Time)	L / R	Bottle (oz.)

Diapers

Wet	Dirty
☐	☐
☐	☐
☐	☐
☐	☐
☐	☐
☐	☐
☐	☐
☐	☐

Tummy Time

Start Time	End Time

Sleep/Naps

Start Time	End Time

Medications

Time	Name & Dosage

Notes

BABY CARE JOURNAL

NAME: _____   DATE: _____

FEEDING

Time	Breast (Time)	L / R	Bottle (oz.)

DIAPERS

Wet	Dirty
☐	☐
☐	☐
☐	☐
☐	☐
☐	☐
☐	☐
☐	☐
☐	☐

TUMMY TIME

Start Time	End Time

SLEEP/NAPS

Start Time	End Time

MEDICATIONS

Time	Name & Dosage

NOTES

Baby Care Journal

NAME: _____ DATE: _____

Feeding

Time	Breast (Time)	L / R	Bottle (oz.)

Diapers

Wet	Dirty
☐	☐
☐	☐
☐	☐
☐	☐
☐	☐
☐	☐
☐	☐
☐	☐

Tummy Time

Start Time	End Time

Sleep/Naps

Start Time	End Time

Medications

Time	Name & Dosage

Notes

Baby Care Journal

Name: _____ Date: _____

Feeding

Time	Breast (Time)	L / R	Bottle (oz.)

Diapers

Wet	Dirty

Tummy Time

Start Time	End Time

Sleep/Naps

Start Time	End Time

Medications

Time	Name & Dosage

Notes

BABY CARE JOURNAL

NAME: _____   DATE: _____

FEEDING

TIME	BREAST (TIME)	L / R	BOTTLE (OZ.)

DIAPERS

WET	DIRTY

TUMMY TIME

START TIME	END TIME

SLEEP/NAPS

START TIME	END TIME

MEDICATIONS

TIME	NAME & DOSAGE

NOTES

BABY CARE JOURNAL

NAME: _____ DATE: _____

FEEDING

Time	Breast (Time)	L / R	Bottle (oz.)

DIAPERS

Wet	Dirty
☐	☐
☐	☐
☐	☐
☐	☐
☐	☐
☐	☐
☐	☐
☐	☐

TUMMY TIME

Start Time	End Time

SLEEP/NAPS

Start Time	End Time

MEDICATIONS

Time	Name & Dosage

NOTES

Baby Care Journal

Name: _____   Date: _____

Feeding

Time	Breast (Time) L / R	Bottle (oz.)

Diapers

Wet	Dirty
☐	☐
☐	☐
☐	☐
☐	☐
☐	☐
☐	☐
☐	☐
☐	☐

Tummy Time

Start Time	End Time

Sleep/Naps

Start Time	End Time

Medications

Time	Name & Dosage

Notes

BABY CARE JOURNAL

NAME: _____   DATE: _____

FEEDING

TIME	BREAST (TIME)	L / R	BOTTLE (OZ.)

DIAPERS

WET	DIRTY
☐	☐
☐	☐
☐	☐
☐	☐
☐	☐
☐	☐
☐	☐
☐	☐

TUMMY TIME

START TIME	END TIME

SLEEP/NAPS

START TIME	END TIME

MEDICATIONS

TIME	NAME & DOSAGE

NOTES

Baby Care Journal

Name: _____   Date: _____

Feeding

Time	Breast (Time)	L / R	Bottle (oz.)

Diapers

Wet	Dirty

Tummy Time

Start Time	End Time

Sleep/Naps

Start Time	End Time

Medications

Time	Name & Dosage

Notes

Baby Care Journal

Name: _____   Date: _____

Feeding

Time	Breast (Time) L / R	Bottle (oz.)

Diapers

Wet	Dirty
☐	☐
☐	☐
☐	☐
☐	☐
☐	☐
☐	☐
☐	☐
☐	☐

Tummy Time

Start Time	End Time

Sleep/Naps

Start Time	End Time

Medications

Time	Name & Dosage

Notes

Baby Care Journal

NAME: _____   DATE: _____

Feeding

Time	Breast (Time)	L / R	Bottle (oz.)

Diapers

Wet	Dirty
☐	☐
☐	☐
☐	☐
☐	☐
☐	☐
☐	☐
☐	☐
☐	

Tummy Time

Start Time	End Time

Sleep/Naps

Start Time	End Time

Medications

Time	Name & Dosage

Notes

Baby Care Journal

Name: _____   Date: _____

Feeding

Time	Breast (Time)	L / R	Bottle (oz.)

Diapers

Wet	Dirty
☐	☐
☐	☐
☐	☐
☐	☐
☐	☐
☐	☐
☐	☐
☐	☐

Tummy Time

Start Time	End Time

Sleep/Naps

Start Time	End Time

Medications

Time	Name & Dosage

Notes

Baby Care Journal

Name: _____   Date: _____

Feeding

Time	Breast (Time)	L / R	Bottle (oz.)

Diapers

Wet	Dirty
☐	☐
☐	☐
☐	☐
☐	☐
☐	☐
☐	☐
☐	☐
☐	☐

Tummy Time

Start Time	End Time

Sleep/Naps

Start Time	End Time

Medications

Time	Name & Dosage

Notes

BABY CARE JOURNAL

NAME: _____   DATE: _____

FEEDING

TIME	BREAST (TIME)	L / R	BOTTLE (OZ.)

DIAPERS

WET	DIRTY
☐	☐
☐	☐
☐	☐
☐	☐
☐	☐
☐	☐
☐	☐
☐	☐

TUMMY TIME

START TIME	END TIME

SLEEP/NAPS

START TIME	END TIME

MEDICATIONS

TIME	NAME & DOSAGE

NOTES

Baby Care Journal

NAME: _____ DATE: _____

FEEDING

Time	Breast (Time)	L / R	Bottle (oz.)

DIAPERS

Wet	Dirty
☐	☐
☐	☐
☐	☐
☐	☐
☐	☐
☐	☐
☐	☐
☐	☐

TUMMY TIME

Start Time	End Time

SLEEP/NAPS

Start Time	End Time

MEDICATIONS

Time	Name & Dosage

NOTES

BABY CARE JOURNAL

NAME: _____ DATE: _____

FEEDING

Time	Breast (Time)	L / R	Bottle (oz.)

DIAPERS

Wet	Dirty
☐	☐
☐	☐
☐	☐
☐	☐
☐	☐
☐	☐
☐	☐
☐	☐

TUMMY TIME

Start Time	End Time

SLEEP/NAPS

Start Time	End Time

MEDICATIONS

Time	Name & Dosage

NOTES

Baby Care Journal

Name: _____   Date: _____

Feeding

Time	Breast (Time)	L / R	Bottle (oz.)

Diapers

Wet	Dirty
☐	☐
☐	☐
☐	☐
☐	☐
☐	☐
☐	☐
☐	☐

Tummy Time

Start Time	End Time

Sleep/Naps

Start Time	End Time

Medications

Time	Name & Dosage

Notes

BABY CARE JOURNAL

NAME: _____   DATE: _____

FEEDING

TIME	BREAST (TIME)	L / R	BOTTLE (OZ.)

DIAPERS

WET	DIRTY

TUMMY TIME

START TIME	END TIME

SLEEP/NAPS

START TIME	END TIME

MEDICATIONS

TIME	NAME & DOSAGE

NOTES

Baby Care Journal

NAME: _____   DATE: _____

Feeding

Time	Breast (Time)	L / R	Bottle (oz.)

Diapers

Wet	Dirty
☐	☐
☐	☐
☐	☐
☐	☐
☐	☐
☐	☐
☐	☐
☐	☐

Tummy Time

Start Time	End Time

Sleep/Naps

Start Time	End Time

Medications

Time	Name & Dosage

Notes

BABY CARE JOURNAL

NAME: _____   DATE: _____

FEEDING

TIME	BREAST (TIME)	L / R	BOTTLE (OZ.)

DIAPERS

WET	DIRTY
☐	☐
☐	☐
☐	☐
☐	☐
☐	☐
☐	☐
☐	☐
☐	☐

TUMMY TIME

START TIME	END TIME

SLEEP/NAPS

START TIME	END TIME

MEDICATIONS

TIME	NAME & DOSAGE

NOTES

Baby Care Journal

NAME: _____ DATE: _____

Feeding

Time	Breast (Time)	L / R	Bottle (oz.)

Diapers

Wet	Dirty
☐	☐
☐	☐
☐	☐
☐	☐
☐	☐
☐	☐
☐	☐
☐	☐

Tummy Time

Start Time	End Time

Sleep/Naps

Start Time	End Time

Medications

Time	Name & Dosage

Notes

Baby Care Journal

Name: _____   Date: _____

Feeding

Time	Breast (Time)	L / R	Bottle (oz.)

Diapers

Wet	Dirty
☐	☐
☐	☐
☐	☐
☐	☐
☐	☐
☐	☐
☐	☐

Tummy Time

Start Time	End Time

Sleep/Naps

Start Time	End Time

Medications

Time	Name & Dosage

Notes

Baby Care Journal

Name: _____   Date: _____

Feeding

Time	Breast (Time) L / R	Bottle (oz.)

Diapers

Wet	Dirty
☐	☐
☐	☐
☐	☐
☐	☐
☐	☐
☐	☐
☐	☐
☐	☐

Tummy Time

Start Time	End Time

Sleep/Naps

Start Time	End Time

Medications

Time	Name & Dosage

Notes

Baby Care Journal

NAME: _____ DATE: _____

FEEDING

Time	Breast (Time)	L / R	Bottle (oz.)

DIAPERS

Wet	Dirty
☐	☐
☐	☐
☐	☐
☐	☐
☐	☐
☐	☐
☐	☐

TUMMY TIME

Start Time	End Time

SLEEP/NAPS

Start Time	End Time

MEDICATIONS

Time	Name & Dosage

NOTES

Baby Care Journal

NAME: _____   DATE: _____

Feeding

Time	Breast (Time)	L / R	Bottle (oz.)

Diapers

Wet	Dirty
☐	☐
☐	☐
☐	☐
☐	☐
☐	☐
☐	☐
☐	☐
☐	☐

Tummy Time

Start Time	End Time

Sleep/Naps

Start Time	End Time

Medications

Time	Name & Dosage

Notes

Baby Care Journal

Name: _____   Date: _____

Feeding

Time	Breast (Time)	L / R	Bottle (Oz.)

Diapers

Wet	Dirty
☐	☐
☐	☐
☐	☐
☐	☐
☐	☐
☐	☐
☐	☐
☐	☐

Tummy Time

Start Time	End Time

Sleep/Naps

Start Time	End Time

Medications

Time	Name & Dosage

Notes

Baby Care Journal

Name: _____   Date: _____

Feeding

Time	Breast (Time)	L / R	Bottle (oz.)

Diapers

Wet	Dirty
☐	☐
☐	☐
☐	☐
☐	☐
☐	☐
☐	☐
☐	☐

Tummy Time

Start Time	End Time

Sleep/Naps

Start Time	End Time

Medications

Time	Name & Dosage

Notes

Baby Care Journal

Name: _____   Date: _____

Feeding

Time	Breast (Time)	L / R	Bottle (oz.)

Diapers

Wet	Dirty
☐	☐
☐	☐
☐	☐
☐	☐
☐	☐
☐	☐
☐	☐
☐	☐

Tummy Time

Start Time	End Time

Sleep/Naps

Start Time	End Time

Medications

Time	Name & Dosage

Notes

Baby Care Journal

Name: _____   Date: _____

Feeding

Time	Breast (Time)	L / R	Bottle (Oz.)

Diapers

Wet	Dirty
☐	☐
☐	☐
☐	☐
☐	☐
☐	☐
☐	☐
☐	☐
☐	☐

Tummy Time

Start Time	End Time

Sleep/Naps

Start Time	End Time

Medications

Time	Name & Dosage

Notes

Baby Care Journal

Name: _____ Date: _____

Feeding

Time	Breast (Time)	L / R	Bottle (oz.)

Diapers

Wet	Dirty
☐	☐
☐	☐
☐	☐
☐	☐
☐	☐
☐	☐
☐	☐
☐	☐

Tummy Time

Start Time	End Time

Sleep/Naps

Start Time	End Time

Medications

Time	Name & Dosage

Notes

BABY CARE JOURNAL

NAME: _____ DATE: _____

FEEDING

TIME	BREAST (TIME)	L / R	BOTTLE (OZ.)

DIAPERS

WET	DIRTY
☐	☐
☐	☐
☐	☐
☐	☐
☐	☐
☐	☐
☐	☐
☐	☐

TUMMY TIME

START TIME	END TIME

SLEEP/NAPS

START TIME	END TIME

MEDICATIONS

TIME	NAME & DOSAGE

NOTES

Baby Care Journal

Name: _____ Date: _____

Feeding

Time	Breast (Time)	L / R	Bottle (oz.)

Diapers

Wet	Dirty
☐	☐
☐	☐
☐	☐
☐	☐
☐	☐
☐	☐
☐	☐

Tummy Time

Start Time	End Time

Sleep/Naps

Start Time	End Time

Medications

Time	Name & Dosage

Notes

Baby Care Journal

Name: _____   Date: _____

Feeding

Time	Breast (Time)	L / R	Bottle (oz.)

Diapers

Wet	Dirty
☐	☐
☐	☐
☐	☐
☐	☐
☐	☐
☐	☐
☐	☐
☐	☐

Tummy Time

Start Time	End Time

Sleep/Naps

Start Time	End Time

Medications

Time	Name & Dosage

Notes

BABY CARE JOURNAL

NAME: _____   DATE: _____

FEEDING

TIME	BREAST (TIME)	L / R	BOTTLE (OZ.)

DIAPERS

WET	DIRTY

TUMMY TIME

START TIME	END TIME

SLEEP/NAPS

START TIME	END TIME

MEDICATIONS

TIME	NAME & DOSAGE

NOTES

Baby Care Journal

Name: _____   Date: _____

Feeding

Time	Breast (Time)	L / R	Bottle (Oz.)

Diapers

Wet	Dirty

Tummy Time

Start Time	End Time

Sleep/Naps

Start Time	End Time

Medications

Time	Name & Dosage

Notes

BABY CARE JOURNAL

NAME: _____ DATE: _____

FEEDING

TIME	BREAST (TIME)	L / R	BOTTLE (OZ.)

DIAPERS

WET	DIRTY
☐	☐
☐	☐
☐	☐
☐	☐
☐	☐
☐	☐
☐	☐

TUMMY TIME

START TIME	END TIME

SLEEP/NAPS

START TIME	END TIME

MEDICATIONS

TIME	NAME & DOSAGE

NOTES

Baby Care Journal

Name: _____   Date: _____

Feeding

Time	Breast (Time)	L / R	Bottle (oz.)

Diapers

Wet	Dirty

Tummy Time

Start Time	End Time

Sleep/Naps

Start Time	End Time

Medications

Time	Name & Dosage

Notes

BABY CARE JOURNAL

NAME: _____ DATE: _____

FEEDING

TIME	BREAST (TIME)	L / R	BOTTLE (OZ.)

DIAPERS

WET	DIRTY

TUMMY TIME

START TIME	END TIME

SLEEP/NAPS

START TIME	END TIME

MEDICATIONS

TIME	NAME & DOSAGE

NOTES

Baby Care Journal

Name: _____ Date: _____

Feeding

Time	Breast (Time)	L / R	Bottle (oz.)

Diapers

Wet	Dirty
☐	☐
☐	☐
☐	☐
☐	☐
☐	☐
☐	☐
☐	☐
☐	☐

Tummy Time

Start Time	End Time

Sleep/Naps

Start Time	End Time

Medications

Time	Name & Dosage

Notes

BABY CARE JOURNAL

NAME: _____   DATE: _____

FEEDING

Time	Breast (Time)	L / R	Bottle (Oz.)

DIAPERS

Wet	Dirty
☐	☐
☐	☐
☐	☐
☐	☐
☐	☐
☐	☐
☐	☐

TUMMY TIME

Start Time	End Time

SLEEP/NAPS

Start Time	End Time

MEDICATIONS

Time	Name & Dosage

NOTES

Baby Care Journal

Name: _____ Date: _____

Feeding

Time	Breast (Time)	L / R	Bottle (Oz.)

Diapers

Wet	Dirty

Tummy Time

Start Time	End Time

Sleep/Naps

Start Time	End Time

Medications

Time	Name & Dosage

Notes

BABY CARE JOURNAL

Name: _____   Date: _____

FEEDING

Time	Breast (Time)	L / R	Bottle (oz.)

DIAPERS

Wet	Dirty
☐	☐
☐	☐
☐	☐
☐	☐
☐	☐
☐	☐
☐	☐
☐	☐

TUMMY TIME

Start Time	End Time

SLEEP/NAPS

Start Time	End Time

MEDICATIONS

Time	Name & Dosage

NOTES

Baby Care Journal

NAME: _____ DATE: _____

FEEDING

Time	Breast (Time)	L / R	Bottle (oz.)

DIAPERS

Wet   Dirty

☐ ☐
☐ ☐
☐ ☐
☐ ☐
☐ ☐
☐ ☐
☐ ☐
☐ ☐

TUMMY TIME

Start Time	End Time

SLEEP/NAPS

Start Time	End Time

MEDICATIONS

Time	Name & Dosage

NOTES

Baby Care Journal

Name: _____   Date: _____

Feeding

Time	Breast (Time)	L / R	Bottle (oz.)

Diapers

Wet	Dirty
☐	☐
☐	☐
☐	☐
☐	☐
☐	☐
☐	☐
☐	☐

Tummy Time

Start Time	End Time

Sleep/Naps

Start Time	End Time

Medications

Time	Name & Dosage

Notes

BABY CARE JOURNAL

NAME: _____   DATE: _____

FEEDING

TIME	BREAST (TIME)	L / R	BOTTLE (OZ.)

DIAPERS

WET	DIRTY

TUMMY TIME

START TIME	END TIME

SLEEP/NAPS

START TIME	END TIME

MEDICATIONS

TIME	NAME & DOSAGE

NOTES

BABY CARE JOURNAL

NAME: _____   DATE: _____

FEEDING

TIME	BREAST (TIME)	L / R	BOTTLE (OZ.)

DIAPERS

WET	DIRTY

TUMMY TIME

START TIME	END TIME

SLEEP/NAPS

START TIME	END TIME

MEDICATIONS

TIME	NAME & DOSAGE

NOTES

Baby Care Journal

NAME: _____   DATE: _____

Feeding

Time	Breast (Time)	L / R	Bottle (oz.)

Diapers

Wet	Dirty
☐	☐
☐	☐
☐	☐
☐	☐
☐	☐
☐	☐
☐	☐
☐	☐

Tummy Time

Start Time	End Time

Sleep/Naps

Start Time	End Time

Medications

Time	Name & Dosage

Notes

BABY CARE JOURNAL

NAME: _____   DATE: _____

FEEDING

TIME	BREAST (TIME)	L / R	BOTTLE (OZ.)

DIAPERS

WET	DIRTY

TUMMY TIME

START TIME	END TIME

SLEEP/NAPS

START TIME	END TIME

MEDICATIONS

TIME	NAME & DOSAGE

NOTES

Baby Care Journal

NAME: _____ DATE: _____

FEEDING

Time	Breast (Time)	L / R	Bottle (oz.)

DIAPERS

Wet	Dirty
☐	☐
☐	☐
☐	☐
☐	☐
☐	☐
☐	☐
☐	☐
☐	☐

TUMMY TIME

Start Time	End Time

SLEEP/NAPS

Start Time	End Time

MEDICATIONS

Time	Name & Dosage

NOTES

BABY CARE JOURNAL

NAME: _____   DATE: _____

FEEDING

TIME	BREAST (TIME)	L / R	BOTTLE (OZ.)

DIAPERS

WET	DIRTY

TUMMY TIME

START TIME	END TIME

SLEEP/NAPS

START TIME	END TIME

MEDICATIONS

TIME	NAME & DOSAGE

NOTES

Baby Care Journal

NAME: _____   DATE: _____

Feeding

Time	Breast (Time)	L / R	Bottle (oz.)

Diapers

Wet	Dirty
☐	☐
☐	☐
☐	☐
☐	☐
☐	☐
☐	☐
☐	☐
☐	☐

Tummy Time

Start Time	End Time

Sleep/Naps

Start Time	End Time

Medications

Time	Name & Dosage

Notes

Baby Care Journal

Name: _____ Date: _____

Feeding

Time	Breast (Time)	L / R	Bottle (oz.)

Diapers

Wet	Dirty
☐	☐
☐	☐
☐	☐
☐	☐
☐	☐
☐	☐
☐	☐

Tummy Time

Start Time	End Time

Sleep/Naps

Start Time	End Time

Medications

Time	Name & Dosage

Notes

BABY CARE JOURNAL

NAME: _____   DATE: _____

FEEDING

TIME	BREAST (TIME)	L / R	BOTTLE (OZ.)

DIAPERS

WET	DIRTY

TUMMY TIME

START TIME	END TIME

SLEEP/NAPS

START TIME	END TIME

MEDICATIONS

TIME	NAME & DOSAGE

NOTES

BABY CARE JOURNAL

NAME: _____   DATE: _____

FEEDING

TIME	BREAST (TIME)	L / R	BOTTLE (OZ.)

DIAPERS

WET	DIRTY
☐	☐
☐	☐
☐	☐
☐	☐
☐	☐
☐	☐
☐	☐

TUMMY TIME

START TIME	END TIME

SLEEP/NAPS

START TIME	END TIME

MEDICATIONS

TIME	NAME & DOSAGE

NOTES

BABY CARE JOURNAL

NAME: _____   DATE: _____

FEEDING

Time	Breast (Time) L / R	Bottle (oz.)

DIAPERS

Wet	Dirty
☐	☐
☐	☐
☐	☐
☐	☐
☐	☐
☐	☐
☐	☐
☐	☐

TUMMY TIME

Start Time	End Time

SLEEP/NAPS

Start Time	End Time

MEDICATIONS

Time	Name & Dosage

NOTES

BABY CARE JOURNAL

NAME: _____   DATE: _____

FEEDING

Time	Breast (Time)	L / R	Bottle (oz.)

DIAPERS

Wet	Dirty
☐	☐
☐	☐
☐	☐
☐	☐
☐	☐
☐	☐
☐	☐
☐	☐

TUMMY TIME

Start Time	End Time

SLEEP/NAPS

Start Time	End Time

MEDICATIONS

Time	Name & Dosage

NOTES

Baby Care Journal

NAME: _____   DATE: _____

Feeding

Time	Breast (Time)	L / R	Bottle (oz.)

Diapers

Wet	Dirty
☐	☐
☐	☐
☐	☐
☐	☐
☐	☐
☐	☐
☐	☐

Tummy Time

Start Time	End Time

Sleep/Naps

Start Time	End Time

Medications

Time	Name & Dosage

Notes

Baby Care Journal

NAME: _____   DATE: _____

FEEDING

Time	Breast (Time)	L / R	Bottle (oz.)

DIAPERS

Wet	Dirty
☐	☐
☐	☐
☐	☐
☐	☐
☐	☐
☐	☐
☐	☐
☐	☐

TUMMY TIME

Start Time	End Time

SLEEP/NAPS

Start Time	End Time

MEDICATIONS

Time	Name & Dosage

NOTES

Baby Care Journal

NAME: _____   DATE: _____

Feeding

Time	Breast (Time)	L / R	Bottle (oz.)

Diapers

Wet	Dirty

Tummy Time

Start Time	End Time

Sleep/Naps

Start Time	End Time

Medications

Time	Name & Dosage

Notes

BABY CARE JOURNAL

NAME: _____ DATE: _____

FEEDING

Time	Breast (Time)	L / R	Bottle (oz.)

DIAPERS

Wet	Dirty
☐	☐
☐	☐
☐	☐
☐	☐
☐	☐
☐	☐
☐	☐
☐	☐

TUMMY TIME

Start Time	End Time

SLEEP/NAPS

Start Time	End Time

MEDICATIONS

Time	Name & Dosage

NOTES

Baby Care Journal

Name: _____   Date: _____

Feeding

Time	Breast (Time)	L / R	Bottle (oz.)

Diapers

Wet	Dirty
☐	☐
☐	☐
☐	☐
☐	☐
☐	☐
☐	☐
☐	☐
☐	☐

Tummy Time

Start Time	End Time

Sleep/Naps

Start Time	End Time

Medications

Time	Name & Dosage

Notes

Baby Care Journal

Name: _____ Date: _____

Feeding

Time	Breast (Time)	L / R	Bottle (oz.)

Diapers

Wet	Dirty
☐	☐
☐	☐
☐	☐
☐	☐
☐	☐
☐	☐
☐	☐
☐	☐

Tummy Time

Start Time	End Time

Sleep/Naps

Start Time	End Time

Medications

Time	Name & Dosage

Notes

Baby Care Journal

Name: _____ Date: _____

Feeding

Time	Breast (Time)	L / R	Bottle (oz.)

Diapers

Wet	Dirty

Tummy Time

Start Time	End Time

Sleep/Naps

Start Time	End Time

Medications

Time	Name & Dosage

Notes

BABY CARE JOURNAL

NAME: _____   DATE: _____

FEEDING

Time	Breast (Time) L / R	Bottle (oz.)

DIAPERS

Wet	Dirty
☐	☐
☐	☐
☐	☐
☐	☐
☐	☐
☐	☐
☐	☐
☐	☐

TUMMY TIME

Start Time	End Time

SLEEP/NAPS

Start Time	End Time

MEDICATIONS

Time	Name & Dosage

NOTES

BABY CARE JOURNAL

NAME: _____   DATE: _____

FEEDING

TIME	BREAST (TIME)	L / R	BOTTLE (OZ.)

DIAPERS

WET	DIRTY

TUMMY TIME

START TIME	END TIME

SLEEP/NAPS

START TIME	END TIME

MEDICATIONS

TIME	NAME & DOSAGE

NOTES

BABY CARE JOURNAL

NAME: _____   DATE: _____

FEEDING

TIME	BREAST (TIME)	L / R	BOTTLE (OZ.)

DIAPERS

WET	DIRTY
☐	☐
☐	☐
☐	☐
☐	☐
☐	☐
☐	☐
☐	☐
☐	☐

TUMMY TIME

START TIME	END TIME

SLEEP/NAPS

START TIME	END TIME

MEDICATIONS

TIME	NAME & DOSAGE

NOTES

BABY CARE JOURNAL

NAME: _____   DATE: _____

FEEDING

Time	Breast (Time)	L / R	Bottle (oz.)

DIAPERS

Wet	Dirty

TUMMY TIME

Start Time	End Time

SLEEP/NAPS

Start Time	End Time

MEDICATIONS

Time	Name & Dosage

NOTES

BABY CARE JOURNAL

NAME: _____   DATE: _____

FEEDING

TIME	BREAST (TIME)	L / R	BOTTLE (OZ.)

DIAPERS

WET	DIRTY

TUMMY TIME

START TIME	END TIME

SLEEP/NAPS

START TIME	END TIME

MEDICATIONS

TIME	NAME & DOSAGE

NOTES

Baby Care Journal

Name: _____   Date: _____

Feeding

Time	Breast (Time)	L / R	Bottle (oz.)

Diapers

Wet	Dirty
☐	☐
☐	☐
☐	☐
☐	☐
☐	☐
☐	☐
☐	☐
☐	☐

Tummy Time

Start Time	End Time

Sleep/Naps

Start Time	End Time

Medications

Time	Name & Dosage

Notes

Baby Care Journal

Name: _____   Date: _____

Feeding

Time	Breast (Time)	L / R	Bottle (oz.)

Diapers

Wet	Dirty
☐	☐
☐	☐
☐	☐
☐	☐
☐	☐
☐	☐
☐	☐
☐	☐

Tummy Time

Start Time	End Time

Sleep/Naps

Start Time	End Time

Medications

Time	Name & Dosage

Notes

BABY CARE JOURNAL

NAME: _____ DATE: _____

FEEDING

TIME	BREAST (TIME)	L / R	BOTTLE (OZ.)

DIAPERS

WET	DIRTY
☐	☐
☐	☐
☐	☐
☐	☐
☐	☐
☐	☐
☐	☐
☐	☐

TUMMY TIME

START TIME	END TIME

SLEEP/NAPS

START TIME	END TIME

MEDICATIONS

TIME	NAME & DOSAGE

NOTES

BABY CARE JOURNAL

NAME: _____   DATE: _____

FEEDING

Time	Breast (Time)	L / R	Bottle (oz.)

DIAPERS

Wet	Dirty
☐	☐
☐	☐
☐	☐
☐	☐
☐	☐
☐	☐
☐	☐
☐	☐

TUMMY TIME

Start Time	End Time

SLEEP/NAPS

Start Time	End Time

MEDICATIONS

Time	Name & Dosage

NOTES

Baby Care Journal

Name: _____   Date: _____

Feeding

Time	Breast (Time)	L / R	Bottle (oz.)

Diapers

Wet	Dirty
☐	☐
☐	☐
☐	☐
☐	☐
☐	☐
☐	☐
☐	☐
☐	☐

Tummy Time

Start Time	End Time

Sleep/Naps

Start Time	End Time

Medications

Time	Name & Dosage

Notes

Baby Care Journal

Name: _____   Date: _____

Feeding

Time	Breast (Time)	L / R	Bottle (oz.)

Diapers

Wet	Dirty
☐	☐
☐	☐
☐	☐
☐	☐
☐	☐
☐	☐
☐	☐
☐	☐

Tummy Time

Start Time	End Time

Sleep/Naps

Start Time	End Time

Medications

Time	Name & Dosage

Notes

Baby Care Journal

NAME: _____   DATE: _____

Feeding

Time	Breast (Time)	L / R	Bottle (oz.)

Diapers

Wet	Dirty
☐	☐
☐	☐
☐	☐
☐	☐
☐	☐
☐	☐
☐	☐

Tummy Time

Start Time	End Time

Sleep/Naps

Start Time	End Time

Medications

Time	Name & Dosage

Notes

BABY CARE JOURNAL

NAME: _____ DATE: _____

FEEDING

TIME	BREAST (TIME)	L / R	BOTTLE (OZ.)

DIAPERS

WET	DIRTY
☐	☐
☐	☐
☐	☐
☐	☐
☐	☐
☐	☐
☐	☐

TUMMY TIME

START TIME	END TIME

SLEEP/NAPS

START TIME	END TIME

MEDICATIONS

TIME	NAME & DOSAGE

NOTES

BABY CARE JOURNAL

NAME: _____ DATE: _____

FEEDING

TIME	BREAST (TIME)	L / R	BOTTLE (OZ.)

DIAPERS

WET	DIRTY
☐	☐
☐	☐
☐	☐
☐	☐
☐	☐
☐	☐
☐	☐
☐	☐

TUMMY TIME

START TIME	END TIME

SLEEP/NAPS

START TIME	END TIME

MEDICATIONS

TIME	NAME & DOSAGE

NOTES

Baby Care Journal

Name: _____ Date: _____

Feeding

Time	Breast (Time)	L / R	Bottle (oz.)

Diapers

Wet	Dirty
☐	☐
☐	☐
☐	☐
☐	☐
☐	☐
☐	☐
☐	☐
☐	☐

Tummy Time

Start Time	End Time

Sleep/Naps

Start Time	End Time

Medications

Time	Name & Dosage

Notes

Baby Care Journal

Name: _____ Date: _____

Feeding

Time	Breast (Time)	L / R	Bottle (oz.)

Diapers

Wet	Dirty
☐	☐
☐	☐
☐	☐
☐	☐
☐	☐
☐	☐
☐	☐
☐	☐

Tummy Time

Start Time	End Time

Sleep/Naps

Start Time	End Time

Medications

Time	Name & Dosage

Notes

BABY CARE JOURNAL

NAME: _____   DATE: _____

FEEDING

Time	Breast (Time)	L / R	Bottle (Oz.)

DIAPERS

Wet	Dirty
☐	☐
☐	☐
☐	☐
☐	☐
☐	☐
☐	☐
☐	☐
☐	☐

TUMMY TIME

Start Time	End Time

SLEEP/NAPS

Start Time	End Time

MEDICATIONS

Time	Name & Dosage

NOTES

Baby Care Journal

Name: _____ Date: _____

Feeding

Time	Breast (Time)	L / R	Bottle (oz.)

Diapers

Wet	Dirty
☐	☐
☐	☐
☐	☐
☐	☐
☐	☐
☐	☐
☐	☐
☐	☐

Tummy Time

Start Time	End Time

Sleep/Naps

Start Time	End Time

Medications

Time	Name & Dosage

Notes

BABY CARE JOURNAL

NAME: _____   DATE: _____

FEEDING

TIME	BREAST (TIME)	L / R	BOTTLE (OZ.)

DIAPERS

WET	DIRTY

TUMMY TIME

START TIME	END TIME

SLEEP/NAPS

START TIME	END TIME

MEDICATIONS

TIME	NAME & DOSAGE

NOTES

Baby Care Journal

NAME: _____   DATE: _____

Feeding

Time	Breast (Time)	L / R	Bottle (oz.)

Diapers

Wet	Dirty
☐	☐
☐	☐
☐	☐
☐	☐
☐	☐
☐	☐
☐	☐
☐	☐

Tummy Time

Start Time	End Time

Sleep/Naps

Start Time	End Time

Medications

Time	Name & Dosage

Notes

BABY CARE JOURNAL

NAME: _____   DATE: _____

FEEDING

Time	Breast (Time)	L / R	Bottle (oz.)

DIAPERS

Wet	Dirty
☐	☐
☐	☐
☐	☐
☐	☐
☐	☐
☐	☐
☐	☐
☐	☐

TUMMY TIME

Start Time	End Time

SLEEP/NAPS

Start Time	End Time

MEDICATIONS

Time	Name & Dosage

NOTES

Baby Care Journal

Name: _____ Date: _____

Feeding

Time	Breast (Time)	L / R	Bottle (oz.)

Diapers

Wet	Dirty
☐	☐
☐	☐
☐	☐
☐	☐
☐	☐
☐	☐
☐	☐

Tummy Time

Start Time	End Time

Sleep/Naps

Start Time	End Time

Medications

Time	Name & Dosage

Notes

Baby Care Journal

Name: _____   Date: _____

Feeding

Time	Breast (Time)	L / R	Bottle (oz.)

Diapers

Wet	Dirty
☐	☐
☐	☐
☐	☐
☐	☐
☐	☐
☐	☐
☐	☐

Tummy Time

Start Time	End Time

Sleep/Naps

Start Time	End Time

Medications

Time	Name & Dosage

Notes

BABY CARE JOURNAL

NAME: _____   DATE: _____

FEEDING

Time	Breast (Time)	L / R	Bottle (oz.)

DIAPERS

Wet	Dirty
☐	☐
☐	☐
☐	☐
☐	☐
☐	☐
☐	☐
☐	☐

TUMMY TIME

Start Time	End Time

SLEEP/NAPS

Start Time	End Time

MEDICATIONS

Time	Name & Dosage

NOTES

BABY CARE JOURNAL

NAME: _____   DATE: _____

FEEDING

TIME	BREAST (TIME)	L / R	BOTTLE (OZ.)

DIAPERS

WET	DIRTY

TUMMY TIME

START TIME	END TIME

SLEEP/NAPS

START TIME	END TIME

MEDICATIONS

TIME	NAME & DOSAGE

NOTES

Baby Care Journal

Name: _____   Date: _____

Feeding

Time	Breast (Time) L / R	Bottle (oz.)

Diapers

Wet	Dirty

Tummy Time

Start Time	End Time

Sleep/Naps

Start Time	End Time

Medications

Time	Name & Dosage

Notes

BABY CARE JOURNAL

NAME: _____   DATE: _____

FEEDING

TIME	BREAST (TIME)	L / R	BOTTLE (OZ.)

DIAPERS

WET	DIRTY
☐	☐
☐	☐
☐	☐
☐	☐
☐	☐
☐	☐
☐	☐

TUMMY TIME

START TIME	END TIME

SLEEP/NAPS

START TIME	END TIME

MEDICATIONS

TIME	NAME & DOSAGE

NOTES

Baby Care Journal

Name: _____ Date: _____

Feeding

Time	Breast (Time)	L / R	Bottle (oz.)

Diapers

Wet	Dirty
☐	☐
☐	☐
☐	☐
☐	☐
☐	☐
☐	☐
☐	☐
☐	☐

Tummy Time

Start Time	End Time

Sleep/Naps

Start Time	End Time

Medications

Time	Name & Dosage

Notes

BABY CARE JOURNAL

NAME: _____   DATE: _____

FEEDING

TIME	BREAST (TIME)	L / R	BOTTLE (OZ.)

DIAPERS

WET	DIRTY

TUMMY TIME

START TIME	END TIME

SLEEP/NAPS

START TIME	END TIME

MEDICATIONS

TIME	NAME & DOSAGE

NOTES

Baby Care Journal

Name: _____   Date: _____

Feeding

Time	Breast (Time)	L / R	Bottle (Oz.)

Diapers

Wet	Dirty

Tummy Time

Start Time	End Time

Sleep/Naps

Start Time	End Time

Medications

Time	Name & Dosage

Notes

Baby Care Journal

Name: _____   Date: _____

Feeding

Time	Breast (Time)	L / R	Bottle (Oz.)

Diapers

Wet	Dirty

Tummy Time

Start Time	End Time

Sleep/Naps

Start Time	End Time

Medications

Time	Name & Dosage

Notes

Baby Care Journal

Name: _____   Date: _____

Feeding

Time	Breast (Time)	L / R	Bottle (oz.)

Diapers

Wet	Dirty
☐	☐
☐	☐
☐	☐
☐	☐
☐	☐
☐	☐
☐	☐
☐	☐

Tummy Time

Start Time	End Time

Sleep/Naps

Start Time	End Time

Medications

Time	Name & Dosage

Notes

BABY CARE JOURNAL

NAME: _____ DATE: _____

FEEDING

TIME	BREAST (TIME)	L / R	BOTTLE (OZ.)

DIAPERS

WET	DIRTY
☐	☐
☐	☐
☐	☐
☐	☐
☐	☐
☐	☐
☐	☐
☐	☐

TUMMY TIME

START TIME	END TIME

SLEEP/NAPS

START TIME	END TIME

MEDICATIONS

TIME	NAME & DOSAGE

NOTES

Baby Care Journal

Name: _____ Date: _____

Feeding

Time	Breast (Time)	L / R	Bottle (oz.)

Diapers

Wet	Dirty
☐	☐
☐	☐
☐	☐
☐	☐
☐	☐
☐	☐
☐	☐

Tummy Time

Start Time	End Time

Sleep/Naps

Start Time	End Time

Medications

Time	Name & Dosage

Notes

Baby Care Journal

Name: _____   Date: _____

Feeding

Time	Breast (Time)	L / R	Bottle (oz.)

Diapers

Wet	Dirty
☐	☐
☐	☐
☐	☐
☐	☐
☐	☐
☐	☐
☐	☐
☐	☐

Tummy Time

Start Time	End Time

Sleep/Naps

Start Time	End Time

Medications

Time	Name & Dosage

Notes

BABY CARE JOURNAL

NAME: _____   DATE: _____

FEEDING

TIME	BREAST (TIME) L / R	BOTTLE (OZ.)

DIAPERS

WET	DIRTY
☐	☐
☐	☐
☐	☐
☐	☐
☐	☐
☐	☐
☐	☐
☐	☐

TUMMY TIME

START TIME	END TIME

SLEEP/NAPS

START TIME	END TIME

MEDICATIONS

TIME	NAME & DOSAGE

NOTES

BABY CARE JOURNAL

NAME: _____ DATE: _____

FEEDING

TIME	BREAST (TIME)	L / R	BOTTLE (OZ.)

DIAPERS

WET	DIRTY
☐	☐
☐	☐
☐	☐
☐	☐
☐	☐
☐	☐
☐	☐
☐	☐

TUMMY TIME

START TIME	END TIME

SLEEP/NAPS

START TIME	END TIME

MEDICATIONS

TIME	NAME & DOSAGE

NOTES

BABY CARE JOURNAL

NAME: _____   DATE: _____

FEEDING

TIME	BREAST (TIME)	L / R	BOTTLE (OZ.)

DIAPERS

WET	DIRTY
☐	☐
☐	☐
☐	☐
☐	☐
☐	☐
☐	☐
☐	☐

TUMMY TIME

START TIME	END TIME

SLEEP/NAPS

START TIME	END TIME

MEDICATIONS

TIME	NAME & DOSAGE

NOTES

BABY CARE JOURNAL

NAME: _____   DATE: _____

FEEDING

TIME	BREAST (TIME)	L / R	BOTTLE (OZ.)

DIAPERS

WET	DIRTY
☐	☐
☐	☐
☐	☐
☐	☐
☐	☐
☐	☐
☐	☐
☐	☐

TUMMY TIME

START TIME	END TIME

SLEEP/NAPS

START TIME	END TIME

MEDICATIONS

TIME	NAME & DOSAGE

NOTES

BABY CARE JOURNAL

NAME: _____   DATE: _____

FEEDING

TIME	BREAST (TIME)	L / R	BOTTLE (OZ.)

DIAPERS

WET	DIRTY
☐	☐
☐	☐
☐	☐
☐	☐
☐	☐
☐	☐
☐	☐
☐	☐

TUMMY TIME

START TIME	END TIME

SLEEP/NAPS

START TIME	END TIME

MEDICATIONS

TIME	NAME & DOSAGE

NOTES

BABY CARE JOURNAL

NAME: _____   DATE: _____

FEEDING

Time	Breast (Time)	L / R	Bottle (oz.)

DIAPERS

Wet	Dirty
☐	☐
☐	☐
☐	☐
☐	☐
☐	☐
☐	☐
☐	☐
☐	☐

TUMMY TIME

Start Time	End Time

SLEEP/NAPS

Start Time	End Time

MEDICATIONS

Time	Name & Dosage

NOTES

BABY CARE JOURNAL

NAME: _____   DATE: _____

FEEDING

TIME	BREAST (TIME)	L / R	BOTTLE (OZ.)

DIAPERS

WET	DIRTY
☐	☐
☐	☐
☐	☐
☐	☐
☐	☐
☐	☐
☐	☐

TUMMY TIME

START TIME	END TIME

SLEEP/NAPS

START TIME	END TIME

MEDICATIONS

TIME	NAME & DOSAGE

NOTES

Baby Care Journal

Name: _____   Date: _____

Feeding

Time	Breast (Time)	L / R	Bottle (oz.)

Diapers

Wet	Dirty
☐	☐
☐	☐
☐	☐
☐	☐
☐	☐
☐	☐
☐	☐
☐	☐

Tummy Time

Start Time	End Time

Sleep/Naps

Start Time	End Time

Medications

Time	Name & Dosage

Notes

Baby Care Journal

Name: _____ Date: _____

Feeding

Time	Breast (Time) L / R	Bottle (oz.)

Diapers

Wet	Dirty
☐	☐
☐	☐
☐	☐
☐	☐
☐	☐
☐	☐
☐	☐
☐	☐

Tummy Time

Start Time	End Time

Sleep/Naps

Start Time	End Time

Medications

Time	Name & Dosage

Notes

BABY CARE JOURNAL

NAME: _____   DATE: _____

FEEDING

Time	Breast (Time)	L / R	Bottle (oz.)

DIAPERS

Wet	Dirty
☐	☐
☐	☐
☐	☐
☐	☐
☐	☐
☐	☐
☐	☐
☐	☐

TUMMY TIME

Start Time	End Time

SLEEP/NAPS

Start Time	End Time

MEDICATIONS

Time	Name & Dosage

NOTES

Baby Care Journal

Name: _____ Date: _____

Feeding

Time	Breast (Time)	L / R	Bottle (oz.)

Diapers

Wet	Dirty
☐	☐
☐	☐
☐	☐
☐	☐
☐	☐
☐	☐
☐	☐
☐	☐

Tummy Time

Start Time	End Time

Sleep/Naps

Start Time	End Time

Medications

Time	Name & Dosage

Notes

BABY CARE JOURNAL

NAME: _____   DATE: _____

FEEDING

TIME	BREAST (TIME)	L / R	BOTTLE (OZ.)

DIAPERS

WET	DIRTY
☐	☐
☐	☐
☐	☐
☐	☐
☐	☐
☐	☐
☐	☐
☐	☐

TUMMY TIME

START TIME	END TIME

SLEEP/NAPS

START TIME	END TIME

MEDICATIONS

TIME	NAME & DOSAGE

NOTES

BABY CARE JOURNAL

NAME: _____   DATE: _____

FEEDING

TIME	BREAST (TIME)	L / R	BOTTLE (OZ.)

DIAPERS

WET	DIRTY
☐	☐
☐	☐
☐	☐
☐	☐
☐	☐
☐	☐
☐	☐
☐	☐

TUMMY TIME

START TIME	END TIME

SLEEP/NAPS

START TIME	END TIME

MEDICATIONS

TIME	NAME & DOSAGE

NOTES

BABY CARE JOURNAL

NAME: _____   DATE: _____

FEEDING

Time	Breast (Time)	L / R	Bottle (oz.)

DIAPERS

Wet	Dirty
☐	☐
☐	☐
☐	☐
☐	☐
☐	☐
☐	☐
☐	☐
☐	☐

TUMMY TIME

Start Time	End Time

SLEEP/NAPS

Start Time	End Time

MEDICATIONS

Time	Name & Dosage

NOTES

BABY CARE JOURNAL

NAME: _____   DATE: _____

FEEDING

TIME	BREAST (TIME)	L / R	BOTTLE (OZ.)

DIAPERS

WET	DIRTY

TUMMY TIME

START TIME	END TIME

SLEEP/NAPS

START TIME	END TIME

MEDICATIONS

TIME	NAME & DOSAGE

NOTES

BABY CARE JOURNAL

NAME: _____   DATE: _____

FEEDING

Time	Breast (Time)	L / R	Bottle (oz.)

DIAPERS

Wet	Dirty
☐	☐
☐	☐
☐	☐
☐	☐
☐	☐
☐	☐
☐	☐
☐	☐

TUMMY TIME

Start Time	End Time

SLEEP/NAPS

Start Time	End Time

MEDICATIONS

Time	Name & Dosage

NOTES

BABY CARE JOURNAL

NAME: _____ DATE: _____

FEEDING

Time	Breast (Time) L / R	Bottle (oz.)

DIAPERS

Wet	Dirty

TUMMY TIME

Start Time	End Time

SLEEP/NAPS

Start Time	End Time

MEDICATIONS

Time	Name & Dosage

NOTES

BABY CARE JOURNAL

NAME: _____ DATE: _____

FEEDING

Time	Breast (Time)	L / R	Bottle (oz.)

DIAPERS

Wet	Dirty
☐	☐
☐	☐
☐	☐
☐	☐
☐	☐
☐	☐
☐	☐
☐	☐

TUMMY TIME

Start Time	End Time

SLEEP/NAPS

Start Time	End Time

MEDICATIONS

Time	Name & Dosage

NOTES

Baby Care Journal

Name: _____   Date: _____

Feeding

Time	Breast (Time)	L / R	Bottle (oz.)

Diapers

Wet	Dirty
☐	☐
☐	☐
☐	☐
☐	☐
☐	☐
☐	☐
☐	☐
☐	☐

Tummy Time

Start Time	End Time

Sleep/Naps

Start Time	End Time

Medications

Time	Name & Dosage

Notes

BABY CARE JOURNAL

NAME: _____   DATE: _____

FEEDING

TIME	BREAST (TIME)	L / R	BOTTLE (OZ.)

DIAPERS

WET	DIRTY
☐	☐
☐	☐
☐	☐
☐	☐
☐	☐
☐	☐
☐	☐

TUMMY TIME

START TIME	END TIME

SLEEP/NAPS

START TIME	END TIME

MEDICATIONS

TIME	NAME & DOSAGE

NOTES

BABY CARE JOURNAL

NAME: _____   DATE: _____

FEEDING

TIME	BREAST (TIME)	L / R	BOTTLE (OZ.)

DIAPERS

WET	DIRTY

TUMMY TIME

START TIME	END TIME

SLEEP/NAPS

START TIME	END TIME

MEDICATIONS

TIME	NAME & DOSAGE

NOTES

BABY CARE JOURNAL

NAME: _____   DATE: _____

FEEDING

TIME	BREAST (TIME)	L / R	BOTTLE (OZ.)

DIAPERS

WET	DIRTY
☐	☐
☐	☐
☐	☐
☐	☐
☐	☐
☐	☐
☐	☐
☐	☐

TUMMY TIME

START TIME	END TIME

SLEEP/NAPS

START TIME	END TIME

MEDICATIONS

TIME	NAME & DOSAGE

NOTES

Baby Care Journal

Name: _____   Date: _____

Feeding

Time	Breast (Time)	L / R	Bottle (oz.)

Diapers

Wet	Dirty
☐	☐
☐	☐
☐	☐
☐	☐
☐	☐
☐	☐
☐	☐
☐	☐

Tummy Time

Start Time	End Time

Sleep/Naps

Start Time	End Time

Medications

Time	Name & Dosage

Notes

Baby Care Journal

Name: _____   Date: _____

Feeding

Time	Breast (Time)	L / R	Bottle (oz.)

Diapers

Wet	Dirty

Tummy Time

Start Time	End Time

Sleep/Naps

Start Time	End Time

Medications

Time	Name & Dosage

Notes

Baby Care Journal

NAME: _____   DATE: _____

FEEDING

Time	Breast (Time)	L / R	Bottle (oz.)

DIAPERS

Wet	Dirty

TUMMY TIME

Start Time	End Time

SLEEP/NAPS

Start Time	End Time

MEDICATIONS

Time	Name & Dosage

NOTES

Baby Care Journal

Name: _____   Date: _____

Feeding

Time	Breast (Time)	L / R	Bottle (oz.)

Diapers

Wet	Dirty
☐	☐
☐	☐
☐	☐
☐	☐
☐	☐
☐	☐
☐	☐
☐	☐

Tummy Time

Start Time	End Time

Sleep/Naps

Start Time	End Time

Medications

Time	Name & Dosage

Notes

Baby Care Journal

Name: _____   Date: _____

Feeding

Time	Breast (Time)	L / R	Bottle (Oz.)

Diapers

Wet	Dirty
☐	☐
☐	☐
☐	☐
☐	☐
☐	☐
☐	☐
☐	☐

Tummy Time

Start Time	End Time

Sleep/Naps

Start Time	End Time

Medications

Time	Name & Dosage

Notes

Baby Care Journal

Name: _____   Date: _____

Feeding

Time	Breast (Time)	L / R	Bottle (oz.)

Diapers

Wet	Dirty
☐	☐
☐	☐
☐	☐
☐	☐
☐	☐
☐	☐
☐	☐
☐	☐

Tummy Time

Start Time	End Time

Sleep/Naps

Start Time	End Time

Medications

Time	Name & Dosage

Notes

BABY CARE JOURNAL

NAME: _____   DATE: _____

FEEDING

TIME	BREAST (TIME)	L / R	BOTTLE (OZ.)

DIAPERS

WET	DIRTY
☐	☐
☐	☐
☐	☐
☐	☐
☐	☐
☐	☐
☐	☐
☐	☐

TUMMY TIME

START TIME	END TIME

SLEEP/NAPS

START TIME	END TIME

MEDICATIONS

TIME	NAME & DOSAGE

NOTES

BABY CARE JOURNAL

NAME: _____   DATE: _____

FEEDING

TIME	BREAST (TIME)	L / R	BOTTLE (OZ.)

DIAPERS

WET	DIRTY
☐	☐
☐	☐
☐	☐
☐	☐
☐	☐
☐	☐
☐	☐
☐	☐

TUMMY TIME

START TIME	END TIME

SLEEP/NAPS

START TIME	END TIME

MEDICATIONS

TIME	NAME & DOSAGE

NOTES

BABY CARE JOURNAL

NAME: _____   DATE: _____

FEEDING

TIME	BREAST (TIME)	L / R	BOTTLE (OZ.)

DIAPERS

WET	DIRTY
☐	☐
☐	☐
☐	☐
☐	☐
☐	☐
☐	☐
☐	☐

TUMMY TIME

START TIME	END TIME

SLEEP/NAPS

START TIME	END TIME

MEDICATIONS

TIME	NAME & DOSAGE

NOTES

BABY CARE JOURNAL

NAME: _____   DATE: _____

FEEDING

TIME	BREAST (TIME)	L / R	BOTTLE (OZ.)

DIAPERS

Wet	Dirty
☐	☐
☐	☐
☐	☐
☐	☐
☐	☐
☐	☐
☐	☐
☐	☐

TUMMY TIME

START TIME	END TIME

SLEEP/NAPS

START TIME	END TIME

MEDICATIONS

TIME	NAME & DOSAGE

NOTES

BABY CARE JOURNAL

NAME: _____ DATE: _____

FEEDING

TIME	BREAST (TIME)	L / R	BOTTLE (OZ.)

DIAPERS

WET	DIRTY

TUMMY TIME

START TIME	END TIME

SLEEP/NAPS

START TIME	END TIME

MEDICATIONS

TIME	NAME & DOSAGE

NOTES

BABY CARE JOURNAL

NAME: _____   DATE: _____

FEEDING

TIME	BREAST (TIME) L / R	BOTTLE (OZ.)

DIAPERS

WET	DIRTY
☐	☐
☐	☐
☐	☐
☐	☐
☐	☐
☐	☐
☐	☐
☐	☐

TUMMY TIME

START TIME	END TIME

SLEEP/NAPS

START TIME	END TIME

MEDICATIONS

TIME	NAME & DOSAGE

NOTES

Baby Care Journal

Name: _____   Date: _____

Feeding

Time	Breast (Time)	L / R	Bottle (Oz.)

Diapers

Wet	Dirty
☐	☐
☐	☐
☐	☐
☐	☐
☐	☐
☐	☐
☐	☐
☐	☐

Tummy Time

Start Time	End Time

Sleep/Naps

Start Time	End Time

Medications

Time	Name & Dosage

Notes

Baby Care Journal

NAME: _____ DATE: _____

Feeding

Time	Breast (Time)	L / R	Bottle (oz.)

Diapers

Wet	Dirty
☐	☐
☐	☐
☐	☐
☐	☐
☐	☐
☐	☐
☐	☐
☐	☐

Tummy Time

Start Time	End Time

Sleep/Naps

Start Time	End Time

Medications

Time	Name & Dosage

Notes

Baby Care Journal

NAME: _____ DATE: _____

Feeding

Time	Breast (Time) L / R	Bottle (oz.)

Diapers

Wet	Dirty
☐	☐
☐	☐
☐	☐
☐	☐
☐	☐
☐	☐
☐	☐

Tummy Time

Start Time	End Time

Sleep/Naps

Start Time	End Time

Medications

Time	Name & Dosage

Notes

Baby Care Journal

Name: _____   Date: _____

Feeding

Time	Breast (Time)	L / R	Bottle (oz.)

Diapers

Wet	Dirty
☐	☐
☐	☐
☐	☐
☐	☐
☐	☐
☐	☐
☐	☐
☐	☐

Tummy Time

Start Time	End Time

Sleep/Naps

Start Time	End Time

Medications

Time	Name & Dosage

Notes

Baby Care Journal

Name: _____   Date: _____

Feeding

Time	Breast (Time)	L / R	Bottle (oz.)

Diapers

Wet	Dirty
☐	☐
☐	☐
☐	☐
☐	☐
☐	☐
☐	☐
☐	☐

Tummy Time

Start Time	End Time

Sleep/Naps

Start Time	End Time

Medications

Time	Name & Dosage

Notes

Baby Care Journal

Name: _____   Date: _____

Feeding

Time	Breast (Time)	L / R	Bottle (oz.)

Diapers

Wet	Dirty
☐	☐
☐	☐
☐	☐
☐	☐
☐	☐
☐	☐
☐	☐

Tummy Time

Start Time	End Time

Sleep/Naps

Start Time	End Time

Medications

Time	Name & Dosage

Notes

Baby Care Journal

Name: _____   Date: _____

Feeding

Time	Breast (Time)	L / R	Bottle (oz.)

Diapers

Wet	Dirty

Tummy Time

Start Time	End Time

Sleep/Naps

Start Time	End Time

Medications

Time	Name & Dosage

Notes

BABY CARE JOURNAL

NAME: _____   DATE: _____

FEEDING

TIME	BREAST (TIME)	L / R	BOTTLE (OZ.)

DIAPERS

WET	DIRTY
☐	☐
☐	☐
☐	☐
☐	☐
☐	☐
☐	☐
☐	☐
☐	☐

TUMMY TIME

START TIME	END TIME

SLEEP/NAPS

START TIME	END TIME

MEDICATIONS

TIME	NAME & DOSAGE

NOTES

BABY CARE JOURNAL

NAME: _____   DATE: _____

FEEDING

TIME	BREAST (TIME)	L / R	BOTTLE (OZ.)

DIAPERS

WET	DIRTY

TUMMY TIME

START TIME	END TIME

SLEEP/NAPS

START TIME	END TIME

MEDICATIONS

TIME	NAME & DOSAGE

NOTES

Baby Care Journal

Name: _____ Date: _____

Feeding

Time	Breast (Time)	L / R	Bottle (oz.)

Diapers

Wet	Dirty
☐	☐
☐	☐
☐	☐
☐	☐
☐	☐
☐	☐
☐	☐
☐	☐

Tummy Time

Start Time	End Time

Sleep/Naps

Start Time	End Time

Medications

Time	Name & Dosage

Notes

Baby Care Journal

NAME: _____   DATE: _____

Feeding

Time	Breast (Time)	L / R	Bottle (oz.)

Diapers

Wet	Dirty

Tummy Time

Start Time	End Time

Sleep/Naps

Start Time	End Time

Medications

Time	Name & Dosage

Notes

BABY CARE JOURNAL

NAME: _____ DATE: _____

FEEDING

Time	Breast (Time)	L / R	Bottle (oz.)

DIAPERS

Wet	Dirty
☐	☐
☐	☐
☐	☐
☐	☐
☐	☐
☐	☐
☐	☐
☐	☐

TUMMY TIME

Start Time	End Time

SLEEP/NAPS

Start Time	End Time

MEDICATIONS

Time	Name & Dosage

NOTES

BABY CARE JOURNAL

NAME: _____   DATE: _____

FEEDING

Time	Breast (Time)	L / R	Bottle (oz.)

DIAPERS

Wet	Dirty
☐	☐
☐	☐
☐	☐
☐	☐
☐	☐
☐	☐
☐	☐
☐	☐

TUMMY TIME

Start Time	End Time

SLEEP/NAPS

Start Time	End Time

MEDICATIONS

Time	Name & Dosage

NOTES

BABY CARE JOURNAL

NAME: _____ DATE: _____

FEEDING

TIME	BREAST (TIME)	L / R	BOTTLE (OZ.)

DIAPERS

WET	DIRTY

TUMMY TIME

START TIME	END TIME

SLEEP/NAPS

START TIME	END TIME

MEDICATIONS

TIME	NAME & DOSAGE

NOTES

BABY CARE JOURNAL

NAME: _____ DATE: _____

FEEDING

TIME	BREAST (TIME) L / R	BOTTLE (OZ.)

DIAPERS

WET	DIRTY
☐	☐
☐	☐
☐	☐
☐	☐
☐	☐
☐	☐
☐	☐
☐	☐

TUMMY TIME

START TIME	END TIME

SLEEP/NAPS

START TIME	END TIME

MEDICATIONS

TIME	NAME & DOSAGE

NOTES

BABY CARE JOURNAL

NAME: _____   DATE: _____

FEEDING

TIME	BREAST (TIME)	L / R	BOTTLE (OZ.)

DIAPERS

WET	DIRTY

TUMMY TIME

START TIME	END TIME

SLEEP/NAPS

START TIME	END TIME

MEDICATIONS

TIME	NAME & DOSAGE

NOTES

Baby Care Journal

Name: _____   Date: _____

Feeding

Time	Breast (Time)	L / R	Bottle (oz.)

Diapers

Wet	Dirty
☐	☐
☐	☐
☐	☐
☐	☐
☐	☐
☐	☐
☐	☐
☐	☐

Tummy Time

Start Time	End Time

Sleep/Naps

Start Time	End Time

Medications

Time	Name & Dosage

Notes

Baby Care Journal

Name: _____ Date: _____

Feeding

Time	Breast (Time)	L / R	Bottle (oz.)

Diapers

Wet	Dirty
☐	☐
☐	☐
☐	☐
☐	☐
☐	☐
☐	☐
☐	☐
☐	☐

Tummy Time

Start Time	End Time

Sleep/Naps

Start Time	End Time

Medications

Time	Name & Dosage

Notes

BABY CARE JOURNAL

NAME: _____   DATE: _____

FEEDING

Time	Breast (Time)	L / R	Bottle (oz.)

DIAPERS

Wet	Dirty
☐	☐
☐	☐
☐	☐
☐	☐
☐	☐
☐	☐
☐	☐
☐	☐

TUMMY TIME

Start Time	End Time

SLEEP/NAPS

Start Time	End Time

MEDICATIONS

Time	Name & Dosage

NOTES

Baby Care Journal

Name: _____   Date: _____

Feeding

Time	Breast (Time)	L / R	Bottle (oz.)

Diapers

Wet	Dirty
☐	☐
☐	☐
☐	☐
☐	☐
☐	☐
☐	☐
☐	☐

Tummy Time

Start Time	End Time

Sleep/Naps

Start Time	End Time

Medications

Time	Name & Dosage

Notes

Baby Care Journal

Name: _____ Date: _____

Feeding

Time	Breast (Time)	L / R	Bottle (oz.)

Diapers

Wet	Dirty
☐	☐
☐	☐
☐	☐
☐	☐
☐	☐
☐	☐
☐	☐

Tummy Time

Start Time	End Time

Sleep/Naps

Start Time	End Time

Medications

Time	Name & Dosage

Notes

Baby Care Journal

Name: _____   Date: _____

Feeding

Time	Breast (Time)	L / R	Bottle (oz.)

Diapers

Wet	Dirty
☐	☐
☐	☐
☐	☐
☐	☐
☐	☐
☐	☐
☐	☐
☐	☐

Tummy Time

Start Time	End Time

Sleep/Naps

Start Time	End Time

Medications

Time	Name & Dosage

Notes

BABY CARE JOURNAL

NAME: _____   DATE: _____

FEEDING

Time	Breast (Time)	L / R	Bottle (oz.)

DIAPERS

Wet   Dirty

TUMMY TIME

Start Time	End Time

SLEEP/NAPS

Start Time	End Time

MEDICATIONS

Time	Name & Dosage

NOTES

BABY CARE JOURNAL

NAME: _____   DATE: _____

FEEDING

Time	Breast (Time)	L / R	Bottle (oz.)

DIAPERS

Wet	Dirty
☐	☐
☐	☐
☐	☐
☐	☐
☐	☐
☐	☐
☐	☐
☐	☐

TUMMY TIME

Start Time	End Time

SLEEP/NAPS

Start Time	End Time

MEDICATIONS

Time	Name & Dosage

NOTES

Baby Care Journal

Name: _____   Date: _____

Feeding

Time	Breast (Time) L / R	Bottle (oz.)

Diapers

Wet	Dirty
☐	☐
☐	☐
☐	☐
☐	☐
☐	☐
☐	☐
☐	☐
☐	☐

Tummy Time

Start Time	End Time

Sleep/Naps

Start Time	End Time

Medications

Time	Name & Dosage

Notes

Baby Care Journal

Name: _____ Date: _____

Feeding

Time	Breast (Time)	L / R	Bottle (oz.)

Diapers

Wet	Dirty
☐	☐
☐	☐
☐	☐
☐	☐
☐	☐
☐	☐
☐	☐
☐	☐

Tummy Time

Start Time	End Time

Sleep/Naps

Start Time	End Time

Medications

Time	Name & Dosage

Notes

BABY CARE JOURNAL

NAME: _____ DATE: _____

FEEDING

TIME	BREAST (TIME) L / R	BOTTLE (OZ.)

DIAPERS

WET	DIRTY
☐	☐
☐	☐
☐	☐
☐	☐
☐	☐
☐	☐
☐	☐
☐	☐

TUMMY TIME

START TIME	END TIME

SLEEP/NAPS

START TIME	END TIME

MEDICATIONS

TIME	NAME & DOSAGE

NOTES

Baby Care Journal

NAME: _____   DATE: _____

FEEDING

Time	Breast (Time)	L / R	Bottle (oz.)

DIAPERS

Wet	Dirty
☐	☐
☐	☐
☐	☐
☐	☐
☐	☐
☐	☐
☐	☐
☐	☐

TUMMY TIME

Start Time	End Time

SLEEP/NAPS

Start Time	End Time

MEDICATIONS

Time	Name & Dosage

NOTES

Baby Care Journal

Name: _____   Date: _____

Feeding

Time	Breast (Time)	L / R	Bottle (oz.)

Diapers

Wet	Dirty
☐	☐
☐	☐
☐	☐
☐	☐
☐	☐
☐	☐
☐	☐
☐	☐

Tummy Time

Start Time	End Time

Sleep/Naps

Start Time	End Time

Medications

Time	Name & Dosage

Notes

BABY CARE JOURNAL

NAME: _____   DATE: _____

FEEDING

TIME	BREAST (TIME)	L / R	BOTTLE (OZ.)

DIAPERS

WET	DIRTY
☐	☐
☐	☐
☐	☐
☐	☐
☐	☐
☐	☐
☐	☐
☐	☐

TUMMY TIME

START TIME	END TIME

SLEEP/NAPS

START TIME	END TIME

MEDICATIONS

TIME	NAME & DOSAGE

NOTES

BABY CARE JOURNAL

NAME: _____   DATE: _____

FEEDING

Time	Breast (Time)	L / R	Bottle (oz.)

DIAPERS

Wet	Dirty
☐	☐
☐	☐
☐	☐
☐	☐
☐	☐
☐	☐
☐	☐

TUMMY TIME

Start Time	End Time

SLEEP/NAPS

Start Time	End Time

MEDICATIONS

Time	Name & Dosage

NOTES

Baby Care Journal

Name: _____   Date: _____

Feeding

Time	Breast (Time)	L / R	Bottle (oz.)

Diapers

Wet	Dirty
☐	☐
☐	☐
☐	☐
☐	☐
☐	☐
☐	☐
☐	☐
☐	☐

Tummy Time

Start Time	End Time

Sleep/Naps

Start Time	End Time

Medications

Time	Name & Dosage

Notes

Baby Care Journal

Name: _____   Date: _____

Feeding

Time	Breast (Time)	L / R	Bottle (oz.)

Diapers

Wet	Dirty
☐	☐
☐	☐
☐	☐
☐	☐
☐	☐
☐	☐
☐	☐
☐	☐

Tummy Time

Start Time	End Time

Sleep/Naps

Start Time	End Time

Medications

Time	Name & Dosage

Notes

Baby Care Journal

Name: _____   Date: _____

Feeding

Time	Breast (Time) L / R	Bottle (oz.)

Diapers

Wet	Dirty
☐	☐
☐	☐
☐	☐
☐	☐
☐	☐
☐	☐
☐	☐
☐	☐

Tummy Time

Start Time	End Time

Sleep/Naps

Start Time	End Time

Medications

Time	Name & Dosage

Notes

Baby Care Journal

Name: _____ Date: _____

Feeding

Time	Breast (Time)	L / R	Bottle (oz.)

Diapers

Wet	Dirty
☐	☐
☐	☐
☐	☐
☐	☐
☐	☐
☐	☐
☐	☐
☐	☐

Tummy Time

Start Time	End Time

Sleep/Naps

Start Time	End Time

Medications

Time	Name & Dosage

Notes

BABY CARE JOURNAL

NAME: _____   DATE: _____

FEEDING

TIME	BREAST (TIME)	L / R	BOTTLE (OZ.)

DIAPERS

WET	DIRTY
☐	☐
☐	☐
☐	☐
☐	☐
☐	☐
☐	☐
☐	☐
☐	☐

TUMMY TIME

START TIME	END TIME

SLEEP/NAPS

START TIME	END TIME

MEDICATIONS

TIME	NAME & DOSAGE

NOTES

Baby Care Journal

NAME: _____   DATE: _____

Feeding

Time	Breast (Time)	L / R	Bottle (oz.)

Diapers

Wet	Dirty

Tummy Time

Start Time	End Time

Sleep/Naps

Start Time	End Time

Medications

Time	Name & Dosage

Notes

Baby Care Journal

Name: _____   Date: _____

Feeding

Time	Breast (Time)	L / R	Bottle (oz.)

Diapers

Wet	Dirty
☐	☐
☐	☐
☐	☐
☐	☐
☐	☐
☐	☐
☐	☐
☐	☐

Tummy Time

Start Time	End Time

Sleep/Naps

Start Time	End Time

Medications

Time	Name & Dosage

Notes

BABY CARE JOURNAL

NAME: _____ DATE: _____

FEEDING

TIME	BREAST (TIME)	L / R	BOTTLE (OZ.)

DIAPERS

WET	DIRTY
☐	☐
☐	☐
☐	☐
☐	☐
☐	☐
☐	☐
☐	☐

TUMMY TIME

START TIME	END TIME

SLEEP/NAPS

START TIME	END TIME

MEDICATIONS

TIME	NAME & DOSAGE

NOTES

BABY CARE JOURNAL

NAME: _____   DATE: _____

FEEDING

Time	Breast (Time)	L / R	Bottle (oz.)

DIAPERS

Wet	Dirty
☐	☐
☐	☐
☐	☐
☐	☐
☐	☐
☐	☐
☐	☐
☐	☐

TUMMY TIME

Start Time	End Time

SLEEP/NAPS

Start Time	End Time

MEDICATIONS

Time	Name & Dosage

NOTES

Baby Care Journal

Name: _____   Date: _____

Feeding

Time	Breast (Time)	L / R	Bottle (oz.)

Diapers

Wet	Dirty
☐	☐
☐	☐
☐	☐
☐	☐
☐	☐
☐	☐
☐	☐
☐	☐

Tummy Time

Start Time	End Time

Sleep/Naps

Start Time	End Time

Medications

Time	Name & Dosage

Notes

BABY CARE JOURNAL

NAME: _____ DATE: _____

FEEDING

TIME	BREAST (TIME)	L / R	BOTTLE (OZ.)

DIAPERS

WET	DIRTY

TUMMY TIME

START TIME	END TIME

SLEEP/NAPS

START TIME	END TIME

MEDICATIONS

TIME	NAME & DOSAGE

NOTES

Baby Care Journal

Name: _____   Date: _____

Feeding

Time	Breast (Time) L / R	Bottle (oz.)

Diapers

Wet	Dirty

Tummy Time

Start Time	End Time

Sleep/Naps

Start Time	End Time

Medications

Time	Name & Dosage

Notes

Baby Care Journal

Name: _____ Date: _____

Feeding

Time	Breast (Time)	L / R	Bottle (oz.)

Diapers

Wet	Dirty

Tummy Time

Start Time	End Time

Sleep/Naps

Start Time	End Time

Medications

Time	Name & Dosage

Notes

Baby Care Journal

Name: _____   Date: _____

Feeding

Time	Breast (Time)	L / R	Bottle (oz.)

Diapers

Wet	Dirty
☐	☐
☐	☐
☐	☐
☐	☐
☐	☐
☐	☐
☐	☐
☐	☐

Tummy Time

Start Time	End Time

Sleep/Naps

Start Time	End Time

Medications

Time	Name & Dosage

Notes

Baby Care Journal

Name: _____   Date: _____

Feeding

Time	Breast (Time)	L / R	Bottle (oz.)

Diapers

Wet	Dirty
☐	☐
☐	☐
☐	☐
☐	☐
☐	☐
☐	☐
☐	☐
☐	☐

Tummy Time

Start Time	End Time

Sleep/Naps

Start Time	End Time

Medications

Time	Name & Dosage

Notes

Baby Care Journal

NAME: _____   DATE: _____

Feeding

Time	Breast (Time)	L / R	Bottle (oz.)

Diapers

Wet	Dirty
☐	☐
☐	☐
☐	☐
☐	☐
☐	☐
☐	☐
☐	☐
☐	☐

Tummy Time

Start Time	End Time

Sleep/Naps

Start Time	End Time

Medications

Time	Name & Dosage

Notes

Baby Care Journal

Name: _____   Date: _____

Feeding

Time	Breast (Time)	L / R	Bottle (oz.)

Diapers

Wet	Dirty
☐	☐
☐	☐
☐	☐
☐	☐
☐	☐
☐	☐
☐	☐
☐	☐

Tummy Time

Start Time	End Time

Sleep/Naps

Start Time	End Time

Medications

Time	Name & Dosage

Notes

Baby Care Journal

Name: _____   Date: _____

Feeding

Time	Breast (Time)	L / R	Bottle (oz.)

Diapers

Wet	Dirty
☐	☐
☐	☐
☐	☐
☐	☐
☐	☐
☐	☐
☐	☐
☐	☐

Tummy Time

Start Time	End Time

Sleep/Naps

Start Time	End Time

Medications

Time	Name & Dosage

Notes

BABY CARE JOURNAL

NAME: _____   DATE: _____

FEEDING

Time	Breast (Time)	L / R	Bottle (Oz.)

DIAPERS

Wet	Dirty
☐	☐
☐	☐
☐	☐
☐	☐
☐	☐
☐	☐
☐	☐
☐	☐

TUMMY TIME

Start Time	End Time

SLEEP/NAPS

Start Time	End Time

MEDICATIONS

Time	Name & Dosage

NOTES

Baby Care Journal

NAME: _____   DATE: _____

FEEDING

Time	Breast (Time)	L / R	Bottle (oz.)

DIAPERS

Wet	Dirty
☐	☐
☐	☐
☐	☐
☐	☐
☐	☐
☐	☐
☐	☐
☐	☐

TUMMY TIME

Start Time	End Time

SLEEP/NAPS

Start Time	End Time

MEDICATIONS

Time	Name & Dosage

NOTES

Baby Care Journal

Name: _____   Date: _____

Feeding

Time	Breast (Time)	L / R	Bottle (oz.)

Diapers

Wet	Dirty
☐	☐
☐	☐
☐	☐
☐	☐
☐	☐
☐	☐
☐	☐

Tummy Time

Start Time	End Time

Sleep/Naps

Start Time	End Time

Medications

Time	Name & Dosage

Notes

BABY CARE JOURNAL

NAME: _____ DATE: _____

FEEDING

TIME	BREAST (TIME)	L / R	BOTTLE (OZ.)

DIAPERS

WET	DIRTY
☐	☐
☐	☐
☐	☐
☐	☐
☐	☐
☐	☐
☐	☐
☐	☐

TUMMY TIME

START TIME	END TIME

SLEEP/NAPS

START TIME	END TIME

MEDICATIONS

TIME	NAME & DOSAGE

NOTES

BABY CARE JOURNAL

NAME: _____   DATE: _____

FEEDING

TIME	BREAST (TIME) L / R	BOTTLE (OZ.)

DIAPERS

WET	DIRTY
☐	☐
☐	☐
☐	☐
☐	☐
☐	☐
☐	☐
☐	☐
☐	☐

TUMMY TIME

START TIME	END TIME

SLEEP/NAPS

START TIME	END TIME

MEDICATIONS

TIME	NAME & DOSAGE

NOTES

Baby Care Journal

NAME: _____   DATE: _____

FEEDING

Time	Breast (Time)	L / R	Bottle (Oz.)

DIAPERS

Wet	Dirty
☐	☐
☐	☐
☐	☐
☐	☐
☐	☐
☐	☐
☐	☐
☐	☐

TUMMY TIME

Start Time	End Time

SLEEP/NAPS

Start Time	End Time

MEDICATIONS

Time	Name & Dosage

NOTES

BABY CARE JOURNAL

NAME: _____   DATE: _____

FEEDING

Time	Breast (Time)	L / R	Bottle (Oz.)

DIAPERS

Wet	Dirty
☐	☐
☐	☐
☐	☐
☐	☐
☐	☐
☐	☐
☐	☐
☐	☐

TUMMY TIME

Start Time	End Time

SLEEP/NAPS

Start Time	End Time

MEDICATIONS

Time	Name & Dosage

NOTES

BABY CARE JOURNAL

NAME: _____   DATE: _____

FEEDING

TIME	BREAST (TIME)	L / R	BOTTLE (OZ.)

DIAPERS

WET	DIRTY

TUMMY TIME

START TIME	END TIME

SLEEP/NAPS

START TIME	END TIME

MEDICATIONS

TIME	NAME & DOSAGE

NOTES

Baby Care Journal

Name: _____ Date: _____

Feeding

Time	Breast (Time)	L / R	Bottle (oz.)

Diapers

Wet	Dirty
☐	☐
☐	☐
☐	☐
☐	☐
☐	☐
☐	☐
☐	☐
☐	☐

Tummy Time

Start Time	End Time

Sleep/Naps

Start Time	End Time

Medications

Time	Name & Dosage

Notes

Baby Care Journal

Name: _____   Date: _____

Feeding

Time	Breast (Time)	L / R	Bottle (oz.)

Diapers

Wet	Dirty
☐	☐
☐	☐
☐	☐
☐	☐
☐	☐
☐	☐
☐	☐
☐	☐

Tummy Time

Start Time	End Time

Sleep/Naps

Start Time	End Time

Medications

Time	Name & Dosage

Notes

Baby Care Journal

Name: _____   Date: _____

Feeding

Time	Breast (Time) L / R	Bottle (oz.)

Diapers

Wet	Dirty
☐	☐
☐	☐
☐	☐
☐	☐
☐	☐
☐	☐
☐	☐
☐	☐

Tummy Time

Start Time	End Time

Sleep/Naps

Start Time	End Time

Medications

Time	Name & Dosage

Notes

Baby Care Journal

Name: _____   Date: _____

Feeding

Time	Breast (Time)	L / R	Bottle (oz.)

Diapers

Wet	Dirty
☐	☐
☐	☐
☐	☐
☐	☐
☐	☐
☐	☐
☐	☐

Tummy Time

Start Time	End Time

Sleep/Naps

Start Time	End Time

Medications

Time	Name & Dosage

Notes

Baby Care Journal

Name: _____ Date: _____

Feeding

Time	Breast (Time)	L / R	Bottle (Oz.)

Diapers

Wet	Dirty
☐	☐
☐	☐
☐	☐
☐	☐
☐	☐
☐	☐
☐	☐
☐	☐

Tummy Time

Start Time	End Time

Sleep/Naps

Start Time	End Time

Medications

Time	Name & Dosage

Notes

BABY CARE JOURNAL

NAME: _____   DATE: _____

FEEDING

Time	Breast (Time)	L / R	Bottle (oz.)

DIAPERS

Wet	Dirty
☐	☐
☐	☐
☐	☐
☐	☐
☐	☐
☐	☐
☐	☐
☐	☐

TUMMY TIME

Start Time	End Time

SLEEP/NAPS

Start Time	End Time

MEDICATIONS

Time	Name & Dosage

NOTES

BABY CARE JOURNAL

NAME: _____ DATE: _____

FEEDING

TIME	BREAST (TIME)	L / R	BOTTLE (OZ.)

DIAPERS

WET	DIRTY
☐	☐
☐	☐
☐	☐
☐	☐
☐	☐
☐	☐
☐	☐
☐	☐

TUMMY TIME

START TIME	END TIME

SLEEP/NAPS

START TIME	END TIME

MEDICATIONS

TIME	NAME & DOSAGE

NOTES

Baby Care Journal

Name: _____   Date: _____

Feeding

Time	Breast (Time)	L / R	Bottle (oz.)

Diapers

Wet	Dirty
☐	☐
☐	☐
☐	☐
☐	☐
☐	☐
☐	☐
☐	☐
☐	☐

Tummy Time

Start Time	End Time

Sleep/Naps

Start Time	End Time

Medications

Time	Name & Dosage

Notes

BABY CARE JOURNAL

NAME: _____   DATE: _____

FEEDING

TIME	BREAST (TIME)	L / R	BOTTLE (OZ.)

DIAPERS

WET	DIRTY
☐	☐
☐	☐
☐	☐
☐	☐
☐	☐
☐	☐
☐	☐

TUMMY TIME

START TIME	END TIME

SLEEP/NAPS

START TIME	END TIME

MEDICATIONS

TIME	NAME & DOSAGE

NOTES

Baby Care Journal

Name: _____   Date: _____

Feeding

Time	Breast (Time) L / R	Bottle (oz.)

Diapers

Wet	Dirty

Tummy Time

Start Time	End Time

Sleep/Naps

Start Time	End Time

Medications

Time	Name & Dosage

Notes

BABY CARE JOURNAL

NAME: _____   DATE: _____

FEEDING

TIME	BREAST (TIME)	L / R	BOTTLE (OZ.)

DIAPERS

WET	DIRTY
☐	☐
☐	☐
☐	☐
☐	☐
☐	☐
☐	☐
☐	☐

TUMMY TIME

START TIME	END TIME

SLEEP/NAPS

START TIME	END TIME

MEDICATIONS

TIME	NAME & DOSAGE

NOTES

BABY CARE JOURNAL

NAME: _____ DATE: _____

FEEDING

TIME	BREAST (TIME)	L / R	BOTTLE (OZ.)

DIAPERS

WET	DIRTY
☐	☐
☐	☐
☐	☐
☐	☐
☐	☐
☐	☐
☐	☐
☐	☐

TUMMY TIME

START TIME	END TIME

SLEEP/NAPS

START TIME	END TIME

MEDICATIONS

TIME	NAME & DOSAGE

NOTES

BABY CARE JOURNAL

NAME: _____   DATE: _____

FEEDING

TIME	BREAST (TIME)	L / R	BOTTLE (OZ.)

DIAPERS

WET	DIRTY
☐	☐
☐	☐
☐	☐
☐	☐
☐	☐
☐	☐
☐	☐
☐	☐

TUMMY TIME

START TIME	END TIME

SLEEP/NAPS

START TIME	END TIME

MEDICATIONS

TIME	NAME & DOSAGE

NOTES

BABY CARE JOURNAL

NAME: _____   DATE: _____

FEEDING

TIME	BREAST (TIME)	L / R	BOTTLE (OZ.)

DIAPERS

WET	DIRTY
☐	☐
☐	☐
☐	☐
☐	☐
☐	☐
☐	☐
☐	☐
☐	☐

TUMMY TIME

START TIME	END TIME

SLEEP/NAPS

START TIME	END TIME

MEDICATIONS

TIME	NAME & DOSAGE

NOTES

Baby Care Journal

Name: _____   Date: _____

Feeding

Time	Breast (Time)	L / R	Bottle (oz.)

Diapers

Wet	Dirty
☐	☐
☐	☐
☐	☐
☐	☐
☐	☐
☐	☐
☐	☐
☐	☐

Tummy Time

Start Time	End Time

Sleep/Naps

Start Time	End Time

Medications

Time	Name & Dosage

Notes

Baby Care Journal

Name: _____   Date: _____

Feeding

Time	Breast (Time)	L / R	Bottle (oz.)

Diapers

Wet	Dirty
☐	☐
☐	☐
☐	☐
☐	☐
☐	☐
☐	☐
☐	☐
☐	☐

Tummy Time

Start Time	End Time

Sleep/Naps

Start Time	End Time

Medications

Time	Name & Dosage

Notes

BABY CARE JOURNAL

NAME: _____   DATE: _____

FEEDING

TIME	BREAST (TIME)	L / R	BOTTLE (OZ.)

DIAPERS

WET	DIRTY

TUMMY TIME

START TIME	END TIME

SLEEP/NAPS

START TIME	END TIME

MEDICATIONS

TIME	NAME & DOSAGE

NOTES

Baby Care Journal

NAME: _____   DATE: _____

Feeding

Time	Breast (Time)	L / R	Bottle (oz.)

Diapers

Wet	Dirty
☐	☐
☐	☐
☐	☐
☐	☐
☐	☐
☐	☐
☐	☐
☐	☐

Tummy Time

Start Time	End Time

Sleep/Naps

Start Time	End Time

Medications

Time	Name & Dosage

Notes

BABY CARE JOURNAL

NAME: _____ DATE: _____

FEEDING

TIME	BREAST (TIME)	L / R	BOTTLE (OZ.)

DIAPERS

WET	DIRTY
☐	☐
☐	☐
☐	☐
☐	☐
☐	☐
☐	☐
☐	☐
☐	☐

TUMMY TIME

START TIME	END TIME

SLEEP/NAPS

START TIME	END TIME

MEDICATIONS

TIME	NAME & DOSAGE

NOTES

Baby Care Journal

Name: _____ Date: _____

Feeding

Time	Breast (Time)	L / R	Bottle (oz.)

Diapers

Wet	Dirty
☐	☐
☐	☐
☐	☐
☐	☐
☐	☐
☐	☐
☐	☐
☐	☐

Tummy Time

Start Time	End Time

Sleep/Naps

Start Time	End Time

Medications

Time	Name & Dosage

Notes

BABY CARE JOURNAL

NAME: _____   DATE: _____

FEEDING

TIME	BREAST (TIME)	L / R	BOTTLE (OZ.)

DIAPERS

WET	DIRTY

TUMMY TIME

START TIME	END TIME

SLEEP/NAPS

START TIME	END TIME

MEDICATIONS

TIME	NAME & DOSAGE

NOTES

BABY CARE JOURNAL

NAME: _____   DATE: _____

FEEDING

TIME	BREAST (TIME)	L / R	BOTTLE (OZ.)

DIAPERS

WET	DIRTY
☐	☐
☐	☐
☐	☐
☐	☐
☐	☐
☐	☐
☐	☐

TUMMY TIME

START TIME	END TIME

SLEEP/NAPS

START TIME	END TIME

MEDICATIONS

TIME	NAME & DOSAGE

NOTES

BABY CARE JOURNAL

NAME: _____   DATE: _____

FEEDING

Time	Breast (Time)	L / R	Bottle (oz.)

DIAPERS

Wet	Dirty
☐	☐
☐	☐
☐	☐
☐	☐
☐	☐
☐	☐
☐	☐

TUMMY TIME

Start Time	End Time

SLEEP/NAPS

Start Time	End Time

MEDICATIONS

Time	Name & Dosage

NOTES

BABY CARE JOURNAL

NAME: _____   DATE: _____

FEEDING

TIME	BREAST (TIME) L/R	BOTTLE (OZ.)

DIAPERS

WET	DIRTY

TUMMY TIME

START TIME	END TIME

SLEEP/NAPS

START TIME	END TIME

MEDICATIONS

TIME	NAME & DOSAGE

NOTES

Baby Care Journal

Name: _____   Date: _____

Feeding

Time	Breast (Time) L/R	Bottle (oz.)

Diapers

Wet	Dirty
☐	☐
☐	☐
☐	☐
☐	☐
☐	☐
☐	☐
☐	☐

Tummy Time

Start Time	End Time

Sleep/Naps

Start Time	End Time

Medications

Time	Name & Dosage

Notes

Baby Care Journal

Name: _____   Date: _____

Feeding

Time	Breast (Time)	L / R	Bottle (oz.)

Diapers

Wet	Dirty
☐	☐
☐	☐
☐	☐
☐	☐
☐	☐
☐	☐
☐	☐

Tummy Time

Start Time	End Time

Sleep/Naps

Start Time	End Time

Medications

Time	Name & Dosage

Notes

Baby Care Journal

Name: _____   Date: _____

Feeding

Time	Breast (Time)	L / R	Bottle (oz.)

Diapers

Wet	Dirty
☐	☐
☐	☐
☐	☐
☐	☐
☐	☐
☐	☐
☐	☐
☐	☐

Tummy Time

Start Time	End Time

Sleep/Naps

Start Time	End Time

Medications

Time	Name & Dosage

Notes

BABY CARE JOURNAL

NAME: _____   DATE: _____

FEEDING

Time	Breast (Time)	L / R	Bottle (oz.)

DIAPERS

Wet	Dirty

TUMMY TIME

Start Time	End Time

SLEEP/NAPS

Start Time	End Time

MEDICATIONS

Time	Name & Dosage

NOTES

BABY CARE JOURNAL

NAME: _____   DATE: _____

FEEDING

TIME	BREAST (TIME)	L / R	BOTTLE (OZ.)

DIAPERS

WET	DIRTY
☐	☐
☐	☐
☐	☐
☐	☐
☐	☐
☐	☐
☐	☐
☐	☐

TUMMY TIME

START TIME	END TIME

SLEEP/NAPS

START TIME	END TIME

MEDICATIONS

TIME	NAME & DOSAGE

NOTES

BABY CARE JOURNAL

NAME: _____ DATE: _____

FEEDING

TIME	BREAST (TIME)	L / R	BOTTLE (OZ.)

DIAPERS

WET	DIRTY
☐	☐
☐	☐
☐	☐
☐	☐
☐	☐
☐	☐
☐	☐
☐	☐

TUMMY TIME

START TIME	END TIME

SLEEP/NAPS

START TIME	END TIME

MEDICATIONS

TIME	NAME & DOSAGE

NOTES

Baby Care Journal

Name: _____   Date: _____

Feeding

Time	Breast (Time)	L / R	Bottle (oz.)

Diapers

Wet	Dirty
☐	☐
☐	☐
☐	☐
☐	☐
☐	☐
☐	☐
☐	☐
☐	☐

Tummy Time

Start Time	End Time

Sleep/Naps

Start Time	End Time

Medications

Time	Name & Dosage

Notes

Baby Care Journal

Name: _____ Date: _____

Feeding

Time	Breast (Time)	L / R	Bottle (oz.)

Diapers

Wet	Dirty

Tummy Time

Start Time	End Time

Sleep/Naps

Start Time	End Time

Medications

Time	Name & Dosage

Notes

Baby Care Journal

Name: _____   Date: _____

Feeding

Time	Breast (Time)	L / R	Bottle (oz.)

Diapers

Wet	Dirty

Tummy Time

Start Time	End Time

Sleep/Naps

Start Time	End Time

Medications

Time	Name & Dosage

Notes

BABY CARE JOURNAL

NAME: _____   DATE: _____

FEEDING

TIME	BREAST (TIME)	L / R	BOTTLE (OZ.)

DIAPERS

WET	DIRTY

TUMMY TIME

START TIME	END TIME

SLEEP/NAPS

START TIME	END TIME

MEDICATIONS

TIME	NAME & DOSAGE

NOTES

Baby Care Journal

Name: _____   Date: _____

Feeding

Time	Breast (Time)	L / R	Bottle (oz.)

Diapers

Wet	Dirty
☐	☐
☐	☐
☐	☐
☐	☐
☐	☐
☐	☐
☐	☐

Tummy Time

Start Time	End Time

Sleep/Naps

Start Time	End Time

Medications

Time	Name & Dosage

Notes

Baby Care Journal

NAME: _____ DATE: _____

FEEDING

Time	Breast (Time) L / R	Bottle (oz.)

DIAPERS

Wet	Dirty
☐	☐
☐	☐
☐	☐
☐	☐
☐	☐
☐	☐
☐	☐
☐	☐

TUMMY TIME

Start Time	End Time

SLEEP/NAPS

Start Time	End Time

MEDICATIONS

Time	Name & Dosage

NOTES

BABY CARE JOURNAL

NAME: _____   DATE: _____

FEEDING

TIME	BREAST (TIME)	L / R	BOTTLE (OZ.)

DIAPERS

WET	DIRTY
☐	☐
☐	☐
☐	☐
☐	☐
☐	☐
☐	☐
☐	☐

TUMMY TIME

START TIME	END TIME

SLEEP/NAPS

START TIME	END TIME

MEDICATIONS

TIME	NAME & DOSAGE

NOTES

BABY CARE JOURNAL

NAME: _____ DATE: _____

FEEDING

TIME	BREAST (TIME)	L / R	BOTTLE (OZ.)

DIAPERS

WET	DIRTY
☐	☐
☐	☐
☐	☐
☐	☐
☐	☐
☐	☐
☐	☐
☐	☐

TUMMY TIME

START TIME	END TIME

SLEEP/NAPS

START TIME	END TIME

MEDICATIONS

TIME	NAME & DOSAGE

NOTES

BABY CARE JOURNAL

NAME: _____   DATE: _____

FEEDING

TIME	BREAST (TIME)	L / R	BOTTLE (OZ.)

DIAPERS

WET	DIRTY

TUMMY TIME

START TIME	END TIME

SLEEP/NAPS

START TIME	END TIME

MEDICATIONS

TIME	NAME & DOSAGE

NOTES

BABY CARE JOURNAL

NAME: _____ DATE: _____

FEEDING

Time	Breast (Time)	L / R	Bottle (oz.)

DIAPERS

Wet	Dirty
☐	☐
☐	☐
☐	☐
☐	☐
☐	☐
☐	☐
☐	☐
☐	☐

TUMMY TIME

Start Time	End Time

SLEEP/NAPS

Start Time	End Time

MEDICATIONS

Time	Name & Dosage

NOTES

BABY CARE JOURNAL

NAME: _____   DATE: _____

FEEDING

TIME	BREAST (TIME) L / R	BOTTLE (OZ.)

DIAPERS

WET	DIRTY
☐	☐
☐	☐
☐	☐
☐	☐
☐	☐
☐	☐
☐	☐
☐	☐

TUMMY TIME

START TIME	END TIME

SLEEP/NAPS

START TIME	END TIME

MEDICATIONS

TIME	NAME & DOSAGE

NOTES

BABY CARE JOURNAL

NAME: _____   DATE: _____

FEEDING

Time	Breast (Time)	L / R	Bottle (oz.)

DIAPERS

Wet	Dirty
☐	☐
☐	☐
☐	☐
☐	☐
☐	☐
☐	☐
☐	☐
☐	☐

TUMMY TIME

Start Time	End Time

SLEEP/NAPS

Start Time	End Time

MEDICATIONS

Time	Name & Dosage

NOTES

Baby Care Journal

Name: _____ Date: _____

Feeding

Time	Breast (Time)	L / R	Bottle (oz.)

Diapers

Wet	Dirty
☐	☐
☐	☐
☐	☐
☐	☐
☐	☐
☐	☐
☐	☐
☐	☐

Tummy Time

Start Time	End Time

Sleep/Naps

Start Time	End Time

Medications

Time	Name & Dosage

Notes

Baby Care Journal

NAME: _____ DATE: _____

FEEDING

Time	Breast (Time)	L / R	Bottle (oz.)

DIAPERS

Wet	Dirty
☐	☐
☐	☐
☐	☐
☐	☐
☐	☐
☐	☐
☐	☐
☐	☐

TUMMY TIME

Start Time	End Time

SLEEP/NAPS

Start Time	End Time

MEDICATIONS

Time	Name & Dosage

NOTES

BABY CARE JOURNAL

NAME: _____   DATE: _____

FEEDING

TIME	BREAST (TIME)	L / R	BOTTLE (OZ.)

DIAPERS

WET	DIRTY

TUMMY TIME

START TIME	END TIME

SLEEP/NAPS

START TIME	END TIME

MEDICATIONS

TIME	NAME & DOSAGE

NOTES

Baby Care Journal

NAME: _____   DATE: _____

Feeding

Time	Breast (Time)	L / R	Bottle (oz.)

Diapers

Wet	Dirty
☐	☐
☐	☐
☐	☐
☐	☐
☐	☐
☐	☐
☐	☐

Tummy Time

Start Time	End Time

Sleep/Naps

Start Time	End Time

Medications

Time	Name & Dosage

Notes

Baby Care Journal

Name: _____ Date: _____

Feeding

Time	Breast (Time)	L / R	Bottle (oz.)

Diapers

Wet	Dirty

Tummy Time

Start Time	End Time

Sleep/Naps

Start Time	End Time

Medications

Time	Name & Dosage

Notes

Baby Care Journal

Name: _____ Date: _____

Feeding

Time	Breast (Time) L / R	Bottle (Oz.)

Diapers

Wet	Dirty

Tummy Time

Start Time	End Time

Sleep/Naps

Start Time	End Time

Medications

Time	Name & Dosage

Notes

BABY CARE JOURNAL

NAME: _____   DATE: _____

FEEDING

TIME	BREAST (TIME)	L / R	BOTTLE (OZ.)

DIAPERS

WET	DIRTY
☐	☐
☐	☐
☐	☐
☐	☐
☐	☐
☐	☐
☐	☐
☐	☐

TUMMY TIME

START TIME	END TIME

SLEEP/NAPS

START TIME	END TIME

MEDICATIONS

TIME	NAME & DOSAGE

NOTES

Baby Care Journal

NAME: _____   DATE: _____

Feeding

Time	Breast (Time)	L / R	Bottle (oz.)

Diapers

Wet	Dirty
☐	☐
☐	☐
☐	☐
☐	☐
☐	☐
☐	☐
☐	☐
☐	☐

Tummy Time

Start Time	End Time

Sleep/Naps

Start Time	End Time

Medications

Time	Name & Dosage

Notes

Baby Care Journal

Name: _____   Date: _____

Feeding

Time	Breast (Time)	L / R	Bottle (oz.)

Diapers

Wet	Dirty
☐	☐
☐	☐
☐	☐
☐	☐
☐	☐
☐	☐
☐	☐
☐	☐

Tummy Time

Start Time	End Time

Sleep/Naps

Start Time	End Time

Medications

Time	Name & Dosage

Notes

BABY CARE JOURNAL

NAME: _____   DATE: _____

FEEDING

TIME	BREAST (TIME)	L / R	BOTTLE (OZ.)

DIAPERS

WET	DIRTY
☐	☐
☐	☐
☐	☐
☐	☐
☐	☐
☐	☐
☐	☐
☐	☐

TUMMY TIME

START TIME	END TIME

SLEEP/NAPS

START TIME	END TIME

MEDICATIONS

TIME	NAME & DOSAGE

NOTES

BABY CARE JOURNAL

NAME: _____   DATE: _____

FEEDING

TIME	BREAST (TIME)	L / R	BOTTLE (OZ.)

DIAPERS

WET	DIRTY
☐	☐
☐	☐
☐	☐
☐	☐
☐	☐
☐	☐
☐	☐

TUMMY TIME

START TIME	END TIME

SLEEP/NAPS

START TIME	END TIME

MEDICATIONS

TIME	NAME & DOSAGE

NOTES

Baby Care Journal

Name: _____   Date: _____

Feeding

Time	Breast (Time)	L / R	Bottle (oz.)

Diapers

Wet	Dirty
☐	☐
☐	☐
☐	☐
☐	☐
☐	☐
☐	☐
☐	☐

Tummy Time

Start Time	End Time

Sleep/Naps

Start Time	End Time

Medications

Time	Name & Dosage

Notes

BABY CARE JOURNAL

NAME: _____   DATE: _____

FEEDING

TIME	BREAST (TIME)	L / R	BOTTLE (OZ.)

DIAPERS

WET	DIRTY
☐	☐
☐	☐
☐	☐
☐	☐
☐	☐
☐	☐
☐	☐
☐	☐

TUMMY TIME

START TIME	END TIME

SLEEP/NAPS

START TIME	END TIME

MEDICATIONS

TIME	NAME & DOSAGE

NOTES

BABY CARE JOURNAL

NAME: _____   DATE: _____

FEEDING

TIME	BREAST (TIME)	L / R	BOTTLE (OZ.)

DIAPERS

WET	DIRTY

TUMMY TIME

START TIME	END TIME

SLEEP/NAPS

START TIME	END TIME

MEDICATIONS

TIME	NAME & DOSAGE

NOTES

Made in the USA
Las Vegas, NV
13 October 2023